The POWER of GOD

The POWER of GOD

Written by
Martha (Marti) McNabb

BOLD TRUTH

Christian Literature & Artwork
A BOLD TRUTH Publication

The Power of God
Copyright © 2014 Martha McNabb

ISBN 13: 978-0-9904376-7-3

BOLD TRUTH PUBLISHING
PO Box 742
Sapulpa, Oklahoma 74067
www.BoldTruthPublishing.com
boldtruthpublishing@yahoo.com

Printed in the USA.

Contents

Preface

We are the righteousness of God in Christ Jesus. We are forgiven and our names are written in the Lamb's Book of Life. We will walk through the river of life, and come out dressed in robes made of white linen which represents righteousness. We will live forever and forever with Him. He is the light of our salvation and the bright morning star. He is our crown of glory and we will live with Him forever in the glory of The Almighty. He holds out His hands to His inheritance and they will take the hands of the Lord, and glorify Him in the beauty of His holiness. We will have overcome and will eat of the tree in the midst of the paradise of the Father God forever with Jesus Christ our High Priest, Savior, and King.

I, Martha L. (Marti) McNabb), believe in all that is written in this book called: The Power of God. I have written it to glorify my Father God in Christ Jesus Living in me. The Kingdom of God is within me. I am the righteous of God in Christ Jesus. All who are believers have these qualities in Christ Jesus.

The POWER of GOD

The Power of God will help us to live in the Kingdom of God while we are here on earth.

The power of God's (love, authority, strength and salvation)

The beginning of Israel was Jacob's name changed to Israel. God said to him that he had contended (wrestled) with God and had the power of God and power with men, and had prevailed. The angel of the Lord was overpowered by Jacob. He went and sought God and his favor. God spoke with Jacob in Bethel. God spoke with Jacob and through Jacob.

The firstborn of Jacob (Israel) had might, strength, excellence of dignity, and the excellence of power. Ruben, Jacob's firstborn failed all of these attributes. Ruben defiled his father Jacob. He went into Jacob's, concubine named Balhah.

▶ **We are to observe kindness and justice.** The power of God's right hand shatters our enemies. Jesus is at His right hand. His power overthrows those who rise up against us.

★ **He gives us power to get wealth to establish His covenant.**

The POWER of GOD

Wealth increases His kingdom by converts to Jesus Christ our Savior. We can go where we need to evangelize today. It is not by our power or strength we gain wealth. We relent our power, and earnestly remember that it is the Lord. Let Him be the power.

God's right hand is in power, and shatters the enemy. The Lord is a man of war. He consumes them like rubble. He overcame the pharaoh of Egypt and his soldiers by His mighty hand. God's people (Israel) went safely across the sea on dry land, and the pharaoh's soldiers drowned when the wall of water came down on them.

★ **God is the power over all.** He is the power, the glory and is the majesty in greatness. All that is in heaven and earth is His. He is exalted head over all. All riches and honor come from Him. In His hands is the power to make great and to give strength to all. We are to thank Him and praise Him for His glorious name and those attributes that His name denotes that He has done. He will prepare our hearts to remember the purposes, and thoughts in Israel and in us. We will remember all He has done and all He will do through His Son Jesus Christ forever. In the name of Jesus every tongue shall confess and every knee shall bow. They shall say Jesus Christ is the Lord of Lords and the King of Kings forever.

By His strength and power our way can be made perfect. We can dwell in high places in Him. Our steps will not slip in Him. We must not rebel against the will of God. We will remember the power of our heavenly God as He opened the sea so the Israelites could go across on dry land. We cannot understand the thunder of His heavenly power but we believe in Him as the power and glory of His people forever in Christ Jesus His Son. We believe in the power of the name of Jesus Christ His Son forever. Jesus Christ is our Savior and redeemer, healer and strength. We are healed and made whole by the power of His resurrection.

2

The POWER of GOD

• **Our power is His power.** We are healed by the strength and power He gives us through Jesus Christ our Savior. He is our healer, our strength and our power now and forever.

Wisdom is God's mighty strength by His power. We are wise in our heart if we fear God's judgment, and justice. He is excellent in power. He will not afflict. He delivers us from our afflictions. We can hear His voice during adversity. He will open our ears to instruction and discipline and command we return from our iniquities. He will show us our transgressions and deliver us from them. If we obey we will spend our days in prosperity and our years in pleasantness and joy. All will be done by the power of God's wisdom.

Power belongs to God to increase riches. Set not your heart on them. He is our provider. We will not starve or go without shelter if we trust Him with all He has given us on earth. Pour out your heart to Him and trust Him with all He has given us on earth. Pour out your heart to Him and trust in Him, and He will provide all you need to live a blessed life. Do not trust in oppression, or robbery. The power to gain riches is by God's power. He will see our work and recompense it in His loving-kindness.

★ **He is our refuge.** Seek God earnestly as you thirst for Him in the sanctuary. We will see His power and His glory. Oh! Lord your loving-kindness is better than life. We will praise You with joyful lips.

Remember Him upon your beds, and meditate on Him in the night watches. He has been our help, and under the shadow of His wings we will rejoice. We are spiritual beings in Jesus Christ. He lives in us to the glory of the Father God. We as all God's children go forth in strength in Jesus. We are increasing in victory as we approach the appearance of Jesus Christ before God in Zion. We are anointed to approach God beyond the veil rent by Jesus Christ death on the cross. It was opened for us to go through by His power and strength in us.

▶ **We are to glorify God in Jesus Christ in the sanctuary** of His grace and mercy forever. All this is done spiritually by the power of Jesus Christ living in His people. We can sing Praise to Him all day long. Praises are in the highways of heaven on earth. A day in His courts is better than a thousand elsewhere.

Each of us as children of God shall appear before God in Jerusalem. Our power has increased from strength to strength to be victorious before His throne of grace forever. We will be anointed in the highways to Zion, the mountain of the Lord. There will be pools of rain blessed by God. We will dwell in His presence and be singing His praises all day long.

We will pass through the valley of weeping (Baca). It will be made a place of springs. Early rains will fill it with pools of blessings. Jesus will be our shield to look upon the face of the Father God. We are His anointed. In Jesus we will stand at the threshold of the house of our Father God. We would rather be a doorkeeper than to be in the tents of the wicked.

We are all on the highways of heaven on earth. We should choose to do His will to be blessed while we are here on this earth. If we walk upright, God's Sun and shield will give us grace as a gift and favor for a future of glory, honor, splendor and heavenly bliss.

★ **He will not withhold any good thing from us.** We must trust in Him. We will be happy and fortunate. We will be envied.

We must lean on You, and believe in You, committing all our ways to You. We must be confident without fear or misgiving. You have a mighty arm; strong is Your hand. Your right hand is soaring high. Mercy, loving-kindness and truth go before Your face. You make Your enemies rejoice. You are a powerful loving God toward all people who keep your feast with joyfulness.

If we love You we are in the power of a joyful countenance. The Lord is clothed or robed in majesty and girded with strength and power.

The world is established and cannot be moved. By His power His throne has always been established. We will willingly offer ourselves in the day of the Lord's power. We will be birthed into the beauty of holiness and dressed in holy array. We will be birthed in the morning. We are priests forever in the Lord Jesus Christ. His army will shatter His enemy (kings) in His day of indignation. He will punish nations by His powerful army of priests. He will crush the heads of many lands. He will drink in the brook in the way and will lift His head triumphantly.

● **We will talk of Your glory and talk of Your power.** We as Your works are to praise You affectionately and gratefully confess and praise You as Your saints. Your Kingdom is the power and, dominion endures throughout all generations. Your Kingdom is everlasting. We will meditate on Your glorious splendor of Your majesty and on Your wondrous works. We will declare Your greatness in heaven and in earth.

You will not hold back any good thing from those in the family of faith. When by Your right hand is the power to do so. We are to love our neighbor and, do good to them when it is in our power to do so. God is good to His family so we are to do good to others.

▶ **Death and life are in the power of the tongue.** We eat the life of it. Whatever we say can bring good or bad upon us. By our words we will be condemned or acquitted, justified or sentenced. The word of a king is authority and, power. We cannot say to him what are you doing?

No man has the power over the spirit to retain the spirit. No man has power in the day of death. Evil will overcome those that practice it and it will not deliver them from it. There is a war in our spirits, but we can and are delivered from it by the spirit of God. Our choice should be to do good and be blessed by it with eternal life by God's spirit. He gives us His power when we are lack of strength. Does not matter what age we are as His children, He will increase our strength when we get weak.

His grace and mercy and favor and loving-kindness is sufficient against any danger, and enables us by His power to receive the strength perfectly fulfilled and completed and made perfectly effective in our weakness. We will gladly glory in our weaknesses and our infirmities.

The strength and power of Jesus Christ our Messiah will rest (pitch a tent) and dwell over us. For Jesus' sake we will be well pleased and take pleasure in infirmities, harshness, persecutions, perplexities, and distresses. For in human strength we are weak and we are truly strong (able, powerful in divine strength). The Lord will avenge us from our persecutors by His power in us and over us. For His sake we suffer reproach by unbelievers. We hope to save some by His power in us. We are called by His name.

By His power and wisdom God spoke the world into establishment. By His wisdom and by His understanding and skill He stretched out the heavens. By His power He stores up the winds and brings them forth and makes lightning for rain.

Jacob had power with the Lord. He had power over the angel of the Lord and prevailed. He wept and sought God's power. God spoke with Jacob at Bethel and through Jacob. He dreamed of a ladder set on earth and the top reached into heaven. Angels were ascending and descending. God gave Jacob the land in which he lay on. God told him his offspring would be countless. His off-spring would as the sand and spread to the West and the East and the North and the South. Jacob's ladder was the beginning of Israel. All the families of the earth shall be blessed and bless themselves. Jacob named that place where he slept Bethel; it was called the city of Luz. Before Jacob named it He made a vow to God. God will be with me and will keep me in the way that I go. God gives Jacob food to eat and clothes to wear.

Jacob went to his father's house in peace and the Lord was his God. He set a monument in the sacred place to God and of all the increase of the possessions God gave to him he gave God a tenth of them. The power of God bestowed all of this on Jacob who became Israel.

Micah was full of the spirit of the Lord and of justice and insight. He declared to Jacob his transgressions and to Israel his sin. They rejected justice and perverted all equity. Evil came upon them. They were not protected by God. Heads of Jacob and rulers of the house of Israel were perverting justice and equity in Jerusalem. The power of God left them. Jerusalem became ruins and evil came upon it. The Lord is slow to anger and great in power and by no means overlooks guilt.

★ **God has His way in the whirlwind and the storm and the clouds are the dust of His feet.** He is abundant in loving –kind-ness and truth. Our God is merciful and gracious. He declared this to Moses. He forgives iniquity and transgressions and sin. God is good, a stronghold in the time of trouble. He knows those who take refuge in Him.

Man should not make his own power his god. Our God is the power and the glory forever. God's glory and power covers the heavens. His brightness is like the sunlight. Rays stream from His hand where His power is hidden. *God came from Teman, the Holy One from Mount Paran. His Glory covered the heavens and His praise filled the earth.* There in the sun like splendor was the hiding place of His power as He appeared on Mount Sinai. It represented (Edom). He was from Paran of the Sinai region. His glory covered the heavens and the earth, and the earth was full of His praise.

★ *His ways are everlasting* and **His goings is of old.** He is coming for the salvation of His people. We should rejoice in the salvation of our God. He is our strength and our deliverer. We will have spiritual progress in high places of trouble, suffering and responsibility. With His strength we can stand during terror. He is a victorious God living in us by His spirit. We can rejoice during trouble and distress. Behold! On the mountain are the feet of them, who bring good news, announcing peace.

Celebrate the feasts "O" Judah and pay your vows. We have been delivered from the wicked one (Satan). He will never pass through us again. He is cut off from us completely. The Lord has restored the splendor of Jacob as the splendor of Israel. God changed Jacob's name to Israel. Jacob received the power of God, had power from God, and had power with God as a nation. Joshua brought the people to Israel to be restored. Now Jesus has delivered Israel forever, and the Christians who believe in Him.

God is the glory of a wall of fire around about Israel, and He is the glory in the midst of her. Jesus is the King of Glory, they would not accept. We are to cherish Jesus our Lord as our husband (Ishi). His name is forever. Israel is the tribe of His inheritance.

There will be a ceaseless supply of oil from the olive trees. *Not by might, not by power, but by My Spirit says, the Lord of hosts.* The oil is a symbol of God's Spirit to Zerubbabel who laid the foundation of the temple, and will finish in the latter days. Joshua the high priest and Zerubbabel prince of Judah will be God's instruments of anointing who stand before the Lord of the whole earth. ***His is the kingdom, the power and the glory forever.***

★ **Jesus has the power and authority to forgive sins.** He lives in us now. We can say in His name rise up and walk to the sick because they are forgiven their sins. Jesus gave us the power and authority to do these things in His holy name. When He arose to go to heaven ***He said "Greater things you will do in My name here on earth.*** We need to know the scriptures (The Word of God) which is God's power. Jesus is God's power in us.

In heaven men do not marry nor are women given in marriage. This is God's resurrected state. When we go to heaven we will be like the angels there. God is not the God of the dead but of the living. We need to read the word of God and know what Jesus said in His teachings.

The Sadducees were silenced by Jesus reply about the Scriptures, so the Pharisees tried to test Jesus by asking what the most important or the greatest principle of the commandments was in the law? *Jesus said "You shall love the Lord your God with all your heart and with all your soul and with your mind (intellect). (Matt. 19: 19)* If you honor your father and your mother you love your neighbor as yourself. *(Deut. 6; 5)* This is the greatest (most important principal) and first commandment. The second like it is: You shall love your neighbor as [you do] yourself. *(Lev. 19: 18)* These two commandments sum up the law and the prophets.

The woman who had a hemorrhage of blood twelve years, and had been to many physicians and got worse, touched the hem of Jesus garment, and Jesus felt the power proceeding from Him. The woman's faith had healed and restored her health. Jesus said daughter your faith has made you well. Go in peace and be healed of your affliction. Faith, trust and confidence in Jesus sprang forth from her and restored her health.

People saw the Kingdom of God come in power before they died. They saw the transfiguration of Jesus. God overshadowed Jesus, Elijah, and Moses there in a cloud. God said "This is My Son, Trustworthy Beloved One". Be constantly listening to Him and obeying Him.

Jesus people (His inheritance) will volunteer freely in the day His power. He will shatter kings in the day of His power. He is our Priest forever and will lift up His head.

We will see the Son of Man (I Am). He is seated at the right hand of power (The almighty) and is coming on the clouds of heaven. Jesus is the Great I Am. He is the everlasting dominion, glory, and the kingdom to all the people, tribes and languages. He is the Ancient of Days, God the Father, and the Son of Man. Jesus will be presented to all the people of the earth in all His glory and power. The powers of heaven will be shaken and all the people will see the Lord Jesus Christ the Son of Man coming in the clouds with great power and glory. He will set up His everlasting dominion. This dominion will not pass away and His kingdom will not be destroyed. Jesus has become the King of kings and the Lord of lords.

The Holy Spirit of God, the Power of the Most High God will overshadow with His glory like a shining cloud and a Holy, pure, sinless offspring of God will be born of Mary as Jesus the Son of God the Father. He is sent with great love from the Father God to save the World from sin.

John the Baptist, baptized Jesus in the Jordan River and the Holy Ghost as the appearance a dove came to Him from God the Father. *God said: "This is My Beloved Son in whom I Am well pleased".*

The POWER of GOD

Jesus went into the wilderness for forty days and nights. He was tempted by Satan. He used the scriptures to put Satan in his place. He went back to Galilee full of the power of God, the Holy Spirit. The fame of Him spread over the whole nation. He was honored, recognized by His teachings and was praised in the synagogues' throughout. He spread The Good News of The Gospel. He was anointed to do so.

He set captives free and caused the blind to see. He delivered the oppressed by the power from the Most High God, His Father. He was teaching in Galilee, Judea, and Jerusalem, and the power of the Lord was present to heal. Confidence sprang forth because of their belief and faith. As the children of God our sins are forgiven because we believe and have faith in Who Jesus Christ is and what He has done for us in His death on the cross and His resurrection. We grow in love for Him as we remember all He has done for us. We are empowered by His Holy Spirit.

In the day they lead Jesus to speak to the people, the chiefs, scribes and Pharisees, and the elders and they would not believe. Jesus said: You will not believe. Jesus said: hereafter the Son of Man will sit at the right hand of the power of God.

We as believer are now clothed in the power of God the Father. This is a promise from God. After Jesus was crucified and had risen He told the disciples to stay in Jerusalem and wait for Him to impart the Holy Ghost of God.

We are now empowered to preach the good news of Jesus, and to teach the nations to repent of their sins as Jesus told the disciples they would. We are to witness to all the nations telling them what Jesus did when He was here and what He is doing now in the earth by the empowerment of the Holy Spirit of God the Father in Jesus Christ name. *He said: Go therefore into the entire world tell them about all the things I did while I was in the world. Tell them that I go to prepare a place for them that where I am they may be also.*

★ **In the beginning was the Word,** Who is Jesus and Jesus was with God and the Word was God. In Jesus is life, and in Jesus we are the light of Him. The world did not recognize, Jesus as the light. Those that did, received Him, and He gave them the power to become the Sons of God. We believe in Jesus name and that He is the Light in us by the power of God. The Word became flesh (Jesus) and dwelled among us. We have the glory as the begotten of the Father God. Jesus living in us is full of grace and truth. We are the Light in the world in Jesus Name.

Jesus displayed His power of greatness in glory openly in Cana of Galilee. He turned water in to wine. His disciples believed in Him adhered to Him and they learned to trust in Him.

God spoke to Israel out of fire on the mountain in Horeb. He spoke to them of how He brought them out of Egypt with His glory and by the power of His mighty hand, and His outstretched arm. They heard His voice and still rebelled against Him, and are still rebelling today because they will not believe that Jesus Christ is the Son of God to the entire world. Jesus says to us to be of good cheer, be confident for He has overcome the world. He has deprived the world of the power to harm us. He has conquered the world for us. We should have perfect peace when tribulation of trials and distress and frustration come. Jesus wants us to remember who He is and all He has done for us. He has overcome the world, and we can overcome the world by His power in us.

Jesus is glorified, exalted, honored, and is magnified by the Father, and Jesus in return glorifies, exalts and magnifies His Father and our Father in heaven. He has power and authority over all flesh. We have eternal life in Him forever. He is glorified by the Father God in earth and in heaven. Jesus was with the Father God before the world existed. Jesus is God manifested to us and lives in us as Christians. Israel first then us as the adopted Israel are all children of God the Father through Jesus Christ His Son.

Before Jesus was crucified, He told Pontus Pilate that he only had power to crucify Him because the Father God had given it to him. Jesus said that the one who had delivered Him over to him had committed the greater sin. Jesus was crucified on the day of preparation for the Passover. The Passover is the day Israel was delivered from Egypt.

Paul the man that Jesus blinded in the street to Damascus was the one who publicly demonstrated the scriptures that Jesus was the Christ. Paul was persecuting the Christians before Jesus blinded him on the road to Damascus. We are to publicly display who Jesus is in our lives as Christians.

The Father God set every season and time for everything by His choice and authority, and personal power. We will receive power, ability, efficiency, and might when the Holy Ghost shall come upon us to be witnesses to the ends of the very bounds, uttermost, remote parts of the earth.

Simon the sorcerer bewitched Samaria, saying that he was the great one. They saw him as a great power of God. They believed him for a long time. Philip came along preaching, concerning the things of God in Jesus Christ name. They believed and followed Philip, and men and women were baptized in Jesus Christ name. Simon also believed in the power of God by miracles and signs that were performed in the name of Jesus Christ. Simon continued to spread the gospel with Philip. The people of Samaria received the power of the Holy Ghost also. The power of God heals our bodies and delivers us from evil in Jesus holy name.

The POWER of GOD

A sick man was made well during the time Peter was teaching the people about the power of the resurrection of the dead. Peter was arrested by the Sadducees for using this power of Jesus Christ name. Peter told the rulers that he was doing this in the power of the name of Jesus Christ of Nazareth whom they had crucified and God raised Him from the dead. Peter was filled with Holy Ghost when he told the rulers these things. *Peter said there is no other name given under heaven among men by which we must be saved.* Five thousand people believed in the name of Jesus Christ.

By great power the apostles witnessed of the power of the resurrection of the Lord Jesus and great grace was upon them all. They received abundance and wealth as each needed. It was to be distributed by Ananias and Saphira also, but they kept a part of the wealth for themselves. They lied to the Holy Ghost when it was in their control not to keep the property. God struck them dead for it. God knows our heart and intentions. They are seen by Him always.

Stephen full of the grace and the power of God performed great signs and wonders among the people. His face appeared as the face of an angel. The rulers were not able to cope with the wisdom and spirit by which Stephen spoke. Stephen was later stoned by them. *As Stephen died he said, "Behold the heavens open and I see the glory of God and Jesus standing at right hand of God." He saw and said these things as he died and he said, "Lord Jesus receive my spirit," and he fell asleep.* He had prayed that the Lord would not condemn those who stoned him.

- **We cannot buy the power of Lord.** It comes by His Spirit and His wisdom. *God anointed Jesus of Nazareth with the Holy Spirit (God Himself), and with His power, Jesus went about doing good and healing all who were oppressed by the devil. God was with Him.* We are to witness of this and that God raised Him up to be in power over the whole universe.

● **By faith we have power over Satan.** We have forgiveness and our inheritance is sanctification by our faith in Jesus Christ. Jesus was declared the power to be the Son of God by His resurrection from the dead according to the Spirit of Holiness; He is Jesus Christ our Lord. The Gospel is the power of God and our salvation because we believe. We are the righteousness of God in Christ Jesus. We live by faith to faith. We are righteous and live by faith in all God is by His power in us as a believer.

The invisible attributes of God, His power and divine nature are clearly seen being understood by what has been made and are without excuse. What is known of God honors Him. We are not to speculate, but to give thanks for understanding through all that has been made. We are to glory in our incorruptible God with thanksgiving.

God raised the pharaoh up to demonstrate God Himself. So His power was shown by the pharaoh to proclaim God's name throughout the earth. God did things by His power because of the pharaoh. He caused the pharaoh to let Israel go. God performed many signs and wonders. God defeated the pharaoh. God's power made known was with much patience.

He calls us His beloved Sons of the living God. We are to be vessels of patience and mercy by the power of the Lord God. Jew's and Gentile's are now the sons and daughters of God the Father in Christ Jesus. He triumphed over our enemies by His power, patience and love for all people on Earth. Jesus Christ the Lord is the seed of David declared to be the Son of God. With power Jesus was resurrected from the dead according to the Spirit of holiness. All powers are ordained, established by God. Every person is to be in subjection to the governing authorities established by God. There is no authority except by God. If we oppose authority we oppose the ordinance of God. If we oppose authorities we put ourselves under condemnation. They are established by the power of God. We are to walk in good behavior.

• **We are to abound in hope by the power of the Holy Ghost in joy and peace.** We are to show forth signs and wonders by the power of the Holy Ghost to all the nations on Earth. We are to show the power of God by the Holy Ghost to all people. By the obedience of faith, the Gospel, and preaching it has been established. We are to reveal Jesus Christ as the Revelation Mystery, kept secret so long in past ages. The Word of the Cross is the power of God preached to the foolish. They are perishing because they do not believe. It is the power of God to us who are saved by it. The Cross is the manifestation of the power of God. Jesus Christ by the power of God became to us who believe the wisdom of God. The righteousness of God sanctified us and redeemed us in Christ Jesus. Jesus Christ is the wisdom and the power of God.

The message to the world is to demonstrate the Spirit of God by His power in Jesus Christ name. Our faith is to not rest in the wisdom of men, but to rest in the power of God. The Kingdom of God does not consist in words but, in power. We are to look for the power of God in men who preach the Word. They are sometime arrogant and puffed up. The deliverance of the Word of God is be done by the power we have being in the Lord Jesus Christ. God has shown up the nonsense and the folly of the Worlds wisdom by the power He has given to Jesus Christ His Son.

• **We should come to people in love and a spirit of gentleness of His power.** We are not to be mastered, or enslaved by anything, or be brought under its power. Not all things are good for us. All are allowed, permissible, and lawful. Nevertheless not all things are good for us, profitable or helpful. Our bodies are not intended for sexual immorality. Too much food is not good for us. We are to be saved, sanctified and raised. God raised Jesus our Lord to life by

His power, and we will be raised in the Lord Jesus Christ by God. Our bodies are the members (bodily parts) of Jesus Christ the Messiah. We are the body of Christ by the power of the living God our Father. We are one spirit with Jesus Christ.

Marriage, children, unmarried, virgins, and relationships in general should be under the (authority) power of God. According to His standards written in the Word of God the Bible, we have been bought with a price (Jesus Christ Sacrifice on the Cross); **therefore glorify God in your body**. Doing things God's way in Jesus Christ brings, peace of mind, happiness and joy into our life in Jesus Christ. We all need the will-power to choose the right things pertaining to our life. Our perfection in Jesus Christ causes the incomplete and imperfect to vanish, be void in our life.

The Apostles had the right (power) to have food and drink at the expense of the churches. They also had the right to take a Christian wife along with them. They also had the power to work in order to go about the work of the Lord. They did the work of the Lord of their own free will.

1 Corinthians 9:11-12 says; If we sow the seed of spiritual good, we have the right to reap from the material benefits. When we do not exercise the power of them. We will hinder the work of spreading The Good News of The Gospel of Jesus Christ. We deprive ourselves for the greater good, again; the work of the spreading of The Gospel of Jesus Christ. We endure hardships. We are to share the food from the church, and offerings from the altar as the Apostles of The Gospel of Jesus Christ. The principle of the Lord is to receive maintenance for spreading The Good News of The Gospel. We are trustees, and commissioned to do the good work of spreading The Gospel. We are not to take advantage of our rights and privileges as preachers of The Gospel. We are not to charge for The Gospel. We become all things, Jew and Gentile, so

we could influence others by The Gospel to become faith believers in Jesus Christ. We drink and eat from the Spiritual Rock; He is Jesus Christ. This spiritual food and spiritual drink is produced by the power of God. The Rock is Jesus Christ.

The Spirit of the Lord is now in us to guide us into righteousness so we will not desire, or crave, covet or lust after evil and carnal things. This is what Israel did as they came out of Egypt.

The man was not created from a woman, nor was man created for the woman. Woman was created to be a helpmate. She was created for the benefit of the man. As men and women we are created to please and reverence God. We are to please each other by the power of God as the angels recognize the authority we have over us and in us as men and women of God. We recognize the power and authority the man has over the woman and the authority God has given man. We are all to help each other as God gives us the authority, or the power to do so in a Godly way. We are to use the power God has given us through Jesus Christ to serve God and others. The authority God has given us is to love and serve one another in love and respect with graciousness, and gracefulness. We are to honor and reverence the Lord as we live. Love has great power as we live and walk in Jesus Christ.

We are to serve God in distinctive varieties of service and administration. God inspires and energizes us to function in these areas by the power and the wisdom of the Holy Spirit. The power to speak a message of wisdom, express a word of knowledge and understanding according to the same Holy Spirit. The Holy Spirit is God Himself speaking from our lips these powerful services to others. We have wonder-working power by the Holy Spirit and extraordinary powers of healing others by the Holy Spirit. These are all given and done by God in us. We can show forth miracles and prophetic insight, the gift of interpreting the Devine will and purpose of God. We are to distinguish between true spirits and false spirits spoken in unknown tongues, and interpreting them. All this is done by Jesus Christ the Anointed One, (The Messiah).

God chooses each one of us individually to do what He wants us to administer to the people. God will give us strength and power to do His services. We will raise Him up in glory and honor.

Jesus is the ruler and authority of over every power in The Kingdom of God.

We are to show forth the illumination of knowledge, majesty, and the glory of God magnified in the person of the face of Jesus Christ the Messiah.

We are frail human vessels of earth with grandeur to show forth the light of the Gospel. The glory of the Lord was sown forth a perishable body and raised an imperishable body. A natural body was raised up as spiritual body. If there is a natural body, there is spiritual body. His body sown in dishonor and raised in glory; He was sown in weakness and raised in power. The first man Adam was a living soul. The last Adam became a life-giving spirit. Adam was made an earthly man. Jesus is a man become spiritual from heaven. **We bear the image of the earthly and will also bear the image of the heavenly. Flesh and blood cannot inherit the Kingdom of God.**

The perishable will not become imperishable. At the last trumpet sound we the dead will be raised imperishable and the believer in Jesus Christ will be changed. The perishable must put on imperishable and the mortal must put on immortality. We thank God Who has overcome the sting of death by Jesus Christ our Lord, our victory over death.

• **Therefore be steadfast, immovable, always abounding in the**

work of the Lord. We must know that our work is not in vain in the Lord. This is all achieved by the victory of the cross and the resurrection of Jesus Christ to everlasting life. This is all done in Jesus Christ for our souls. We are saved by a spiritual transformation in life and in death to victory in Jesus Christ our Lord and King.

We should desire that the light of Jesus Christ, and we will shine forth in our hearts the knowledge of the glory of God in the face of Jesus Christ. We should work toward the perfection of Jesus Christ in God our Father. We as earthen vessels have this treasure in us to show forth the surpassing greatness from our Lord God and not ourselves.

We will not be crushed or destroyed by any affliction. We will be persecuted but not forsaken. We will always carry the dying of the body of Jesus Christ that His life will be manifest in our body until He comes for us. By grace we show forth the thankfulness to all people, the glory of God as we live in Christ Jesus by God's power. We should be manifesting the truth of the Word of God commending ourselves to every man's conscience in the sight of God our Father. The glory of Christ Jesus' power is the image of God.

The power of the Lord in us causes us to be renewed day by day. Our flesh is decaying, but our spirit in Jesus Christ will always live. The things that are new are temporal, and Spiritual things not seen are eternal. We will be raised as Jesus Christ was raised into eternal life forever.

In our afflictions we are to cause no offense, so the ministry of the Word of God will not be discredited. We are to have the weapons of righteousness in the right hand and in the left, serving God by showing forth the truth of God's Word by the power of God's Word living in us.

The churches of Macedonia gave liberally out of their abundance of joy in poverty and afflictions to the saints. They supported the saints with all the power and ability they had. They gave themselves to the Lord and to the apostles as the Lord God willed them to. They participated in equipping the saints in love, faith, and utterance in knowledge, all in earnestness.

God wants us to abound in His gracious work by His power in love and grace. He gives us favor to do these things for the support of the Saints. The power of God is made perfect in our weaknesses. His grace is sufficient for us in our weakness. We will go through many afflictions for Jesus Christ's sake. Grace and favor, and most of all His love for us we will show forth His glory liberally in His power.

Jesus Christ was crucified because of weakness, yet he lives because of the power of God. In our weaknesses if we live toward Him, we will have the power to show others his glory. We have the same power abiding in us that raised Jesus Christ from the dead. God has given us the power to edify people, not destroy them as we spread the Gospel. We are to do nothing against the truth, but only for the truth of the Gospel or Word of Jesus Christ in us. God will give us the spirit of wisdom and the re-velation of the knowledge of Him. We should pray that the eyes of our heart will be opened to the hope of His calling. **We are to know what the hope of our calling is and the glory of His riches as His inheritance to His saints (us).**

• **We are to know His greatness of His power toward us who believe.** These are the workings of His mighty strength in us. It is Jesus Christ resurrected and seated at the right hand of God in the heavenly places. He is above all principalities and powers and might and dominions. His Name is above every name in the world and that which is to come. All things are under Jesus Christ's feet. He is the head over all things in the Church. In His resurrected body Jesus Christ our Savior fulfills all in all forever. We as the Church are delivered if we believe, from the power of the prince of the power of the air that is working in the spirit of sons of destruction.

God so loved the world that His mercy is rich toward us. We are dead to our transgressions and made alive together in Christ Jesus. By grace we have been saved and raised up with Him and are seated in heavenly places with Him in Jesus Christ His Son and our Savior forever. He will show us surpassing riches of grace in kindness toward us in Jesus Christ. **By grace we have been saved through faith and that not of ourselves. It is a gift of God.** Jesus Christ is our peace.

We were excluded from the commonwealth of Israel and strangers to the covenant of promise. We had no hope. We were without God in the world. The blood of Jesus Christ brought us together. We are one body to God through the Cross. Now both the ones who were far off (Gentiles) became one with Israel and have access to the Father God by one spirit in the Father. We are no longer strangers and aliens. We are along with Israel of the household of God. We are built together as a dwelling of God in Spirit by Jesus Christ. This is according to the Cross of the power of the resurrection life in Jesus Christ.

We are called to be ministers according to the gift of God's grace which is given to us. We are to be good stewards of God's grace given to us in Christ Jesus. We are growing in to a spiritual building, not built by human hands, and we will be will be the Temple of God in spirit. Our flesh is decaying but the of Spirit of God is growing in us day by day. The Gentiles became fellow-heirs, and fellow members of the body and fellow partakers of the promise in Christ Jesus, through The Gospel.

Therefore we bow down on our knees before the Father God from whom every family in heaven and on earth are named, that He would grant us according to His riches in glory, to strengthen us with His power through His Spirit in our inner man, that Christ will dwell in our hearts by our faith and that we will be rooted and grounded in love. May we be able to understand (comprehend) with all the saints the width, the length, and the height and the depth. We need to know that Christ in our hearts will help us understand that this is the love of Jesus Christ that brings to us the fullness of God. We are to know the love of Jesus Christ that surpasses knowledge and be filled with the fullness of God. The fullness of God is beyond all we can ask or think according to the power that works within us. In Him is the glory in The Church and to all generations forever and ever. A-men...

By God's power we are to strive to become a perfect person to the measure of the stature of the fullness of Jesus Christ. We are to be subject to one another in the fear of Christ our God. Do service to the Lord God and not to men. The Lord is not a respecter of persons. We are regarded equally. **We are to be strong in the Lord Jesus Christ by the power of His might. We are to put on the whole armor of God so we can stand in the day of evil having done all to stand against the devil.**

We are to take up the shield of faith, put on the helmet of salvation, the breast plate of righteousness, have our feet shod with the preparation of the gospel of peace, and our loins girded with the truth. We are to take up the sword of the Word of God. We are to pray in the Spirit at all times so we will be ready to speak the mystery of the gospel in boldness. As an ambassador we can speak for Jesus Christ. We are to be faithful ministers of the Word of God.

Jesus Christ has called us in order that we may obtain the resurrection from the dead. We should be reaching for what is ahead and not behind us toward the perfecting of the saints. This is the righteousness that comes from God on the basis of faith.

We are to worship in the Spirit of God and glory in Christ Jesus and put no confidence in the flesh. We are to get to know Jesus Christ and the power of His resurrection. We press toward the goal of the prize of the upward or the highest calling of God in Christ Jesus. These things come as we obtain the knowledge and know the fellowship of His sufferings being conformed to His death and attain the resurrection from the dead.

We eagerly wait for the return of our Savior the Lord Jesus Christ. We are to understand the grace of God and the truth of Who Jesus Christ is and the power of His resurrection. We are to walk in the love of the Spirit and understand the knowledge of His will in all spiritual wisdom and understanding.

▶ **We will be strengthened with all power according to His glorious might.** We will obtain steadfastness and patience joyously. We are called the Saints of light sharing in the inheritance of the Spirit of Light qualified by the Father God in thankfulness for it. We are delivered from the domain of darkness and transformed and transferred into The Kingdom of God in Christ Jesus His beloved Son.

★ **Jesus is the image of the invisible God. He is the firstborn of creation.** We are redeemed and forgiven our sins forever. The power Jesus Christ in the Father as God Himself created all things in Heaven and Earth visible and invisible, thrones and dominions, rulers and authorities. They were created for Him and through Him. He is before all things and in Him all things hold together by His power. Jesus Christ is the first-born from the dead and has become first place in everything. All fullness dwells in Him in the Father's good pleasure. Jesus has reconciled all things back to the Father by His death on the cross and His resurrection from the dead.

We as ministers of the power of God in Christ Jesus are to administer to every person the wisdom of the mystery of the riches of glory which is Christ Jesus in us the hope of glory. In Christ death on the cross the power of the resurrection will present us before God holy and blameless and beyond reproach in Jesus Christ in us.

We are filled with the Godhead (Father, Son, and the Holy Ghost, God's Spirit). We are in the fullness of life in Jesus Christ (full spiritual stature). Jesus Christ is the head of all rules and authority of every angel, principality, and power.

Our carnal nature with all of its passion and lusts were stripped away. We are not in bondage to them. We are free because Jesus nailed them to His cross of deliverance (freed us) from our sins once and for all. The cross is before us and we leave our sin-full nature behind us. This is for us the freedom and forgiveness forever. We have the power to change as we put the cross before us and we put our carnality behind us.

Our choices are to be God-Ward as we walk in His ways toward a heavenly life in Jesus Christ. Jesus is the head of all principalities and powers in our life. We first have to call out His Name. He is all in all forever.

We should know that the Word of God came to us with great conviction and absolute certainty by the inherent power of the Holy Spirit (God Himself). Power comes to us by the glad tidings of the Gospel of Jesus Christ. We are to imitate the Lord Himself and be inspired by the Holy Spirit of God.

Those that do not know, perceive or become acquainted with God will be excluded and banished from the presence of the Lord and from the glory of His power. May His gracious purpose of gladness and power be complete in our every particular work of faith and wisdom. May our whole human personality in God with absolute trust and confidence in His power become complete in His wisdom and gladness. May we be worthy in Jesus Christ of His calling according to His Holy Sacrifice on the cross.

We are to accept and believe, be marveled at and admired by His glory reflected in us by His power. He is to be glorified and glorious through us and in us according to the grace (favor and blessing) of our God and our Lord Jesus Christ (the Messiah, the Anointed One).

Satan will show forth great power by lying wonders. He is the lawless one the antichrist. Satan will use wicked deception.

We are to love the power of the truth, Jesus Christ. We are delivered from perdition. We are to take no pleasure in unrighteousness. We have received the power in Jesus Christ to be examples before others in Him. In Jesus Christ, the honor and the everlasting power and dominion prevail forever. Amen

• **We are not to have a spirit of timidity, cowardice or fear.** We are to have a spirit of power and of love and of calm, of well-balanced mind and discipline and self-control. We are not to blush or be ashamed to testify to others about our Lord. We do this in the power of God. If we are ashamed of Jesus (not to speak His Name) He will be ashamed of us before the Father God. We are called according to His purpose and grace in our Savior the Lord Jesus Christ. The truth has been entrusted through Jesus Christ in us. We are to teach wholesome and sound teachings. This is for the proclaiming of The Gospel with faith and love to anyone who will receive it and be saved.

We are to avoid people who are strangers to the love of God and the power of it. These are religious people exerted with self-conceit. They take part in the vain amusements of the world. They put these things before God. They are self-seekers. They use God's word for gain and popularity. **Avoid people who have a form of godliness, but deny the power of God.**

★ **Jesus Christ, God's Son is made heir of all things.** God made the world through Him. God the Father and Jesus Christ His Son were side by side creating the world. Jesus is the radiance of God's glory and is the exact representation of God's nature and He upholds all things by the word of His power.

He made purification of sins and is now seated at the right hand of the Majesty of God the Father. He is the master and the power of the universe. Jesus is much better than the angels because He has inherited a more excellent name than they. God did not ever say to an angel: "You are My Son. Today I have begotten you and I will be a Father to you and you shall be a Son to Me". The Father said this to Jesus. Jesus Christ has an official Son-ship relation with God His Father forever. Jesus Christ is King. Jesus Christ Himself makes the angels wind and ministers of flames of fire. God the Father has not ever said to any angel: "Sit at my right hand until I make your enemies a footstool for your feet". God the Father said this to Jesus.

Jesus took on the flesh and nature of a human being. He went through death on the cross that He might bring to nothing and make to no effect the power of death the devil had control of. We are free from the fear of death. Our bodies are spiritual in Jesus Christ who lives in us. Jesus did not reach out to save fallen angels. He reached and saved the desendents of Abraham and delivered them from death. Jesus is our atonement and propitiation for our sins forever. Jesus is the basis for the power of an endless and indestructible life. Unchangeable is His promise and His oath. He will never be proven false or deceive us. We have inherited the promise, the unchangeable. We have the hope of an anchored soul that can enter beyond the veil in Christ Jesus our Savior.

Jesus is our forerunner for us as High Priest forever, according to the order of Melchehizedek. Jesus is our strength and grace as we pass through the heavens in death becoming victorious in Him our King and High Priest forever.

The tribe of Judah was not a part of the Laodicea priesthood. Jesus arose out of the priesthood of the order of Melchizedek. There is a change that came especially for Jesus as the law changed. Judah was another tribe who was not officiated at the altar as the tribes of the Leviticus priesthood was. His is a new beginning as our High Priest in God the Father as the tribe of Judah a Royal Priesthood.

Jesus Christ is our High Priest forever according to the order of Melchizedek, a letter of hope come so we could draw near to God. The law made nothing perfect as Jesus Christ has. He took no oath. God has sworn and will not change His mind that Jesus Christ is our High Priest forever. Jesus is our covenant with the Father God. The Son of God is appointed and made perfect forever. Jesus Christ offered Himself as our sacrifice once and for all. We are made new, born again to a living hope by the resurrection of Jesus Christ from the dead. This is done for us by God's great mercy.

 • **By His power we have an inheritance which will not fade away, reserved in Heaven for us.** A salvation protected by the power of God through faith. It is ready to be revealed in the last day or, time. We have joy unspeakable and full of glory. We love Him though we do not see Him. We rejoice in Him, and believe in Him. The outcome of our faith will be and is the salvation of our souls. We can speak all things by the Holy Spirit sent from Heaven concerning The Gospel. We can speak the things the angels long to look upon.

Jesus called us by His own glory and excellence. His Devine

power has been granted to us pertaining to life and godliness. We have received by His Devine power His precious and magnificent promises. By them we will become partakers of His Divine nature. We will not be corrupted by the world's lusts. We will be diligent in faith and it will supply moral excellence and in our moral excellence we will gain knowledge by that knowledge we will receive self-control, perseverance, and by perseverance we will live in godliness. In our godliness we will live in brotherly kindness. In our brotherly kindness we will live in Christian love. These qualities are not to be useless. They should be increasing, showing forth in our life as truth in fruitfulness in true knowledge of our Lord Jesus Christ. If we are lacking in these we are blinded or short sighted and have forgotten our purification from our former sins. We should be diligent in our certainty of His calling or choosing. As long as we practice these things we will never stumble.

Our entrance into the eternal Kingdom of our Lord, and Savior Jesus Christ will be abundantly supplied to us. We will have moral and excellent knowledge to enter into His Kingdom. We are to be an energized Christian developed in excellence and intelligence.

There are those who revile against angelic majesties and do not tremble when they do. The angels who are greater in might and power do not bring reviling judgment against them before the Lord. These human beings will die like animals that live by instinct. They will be destroyed with the animals because they do not fear God. They are indulgent in fleshly desires, and despise authority and are daring and self-willed.

We will not stumble. Now to Him who is able to keep us from stumbling will make us stand in the presence of His glory with great joy and stand blameless before Him. To the only true God our Savior through Jesus Christ our Lord is the glory, majesty, dominion and power and authority before time and now and forever to all ages of eternity. Amen (So Be It).   If we keep God's command, do His deeds or works as an over-comer, He will give us power and authority over nations.   By the power of His Word and the Blood of the Lamb, and the Cross, we will overcome till the end.

Worthy are You, Oh! Lord our God to receive glory, honor, and power. You created all things, and because of you they have existed and were created.   The twenty-four elders will fall down and cast their crowns before the throne.   They will shout to You, Worthy is the Lamb Jesus, that was slain to receive power and riches and wisdom and might and honor and glory and blessing.

Everything in the earth and on the earth and in the sea says: *To Him, who sits on the throne and to the Lamb, is blessing and honor and glory and dominion forever and ever.*

The Lamb broke open one of the seven seals and there came a white horse and He who was riding carried a bow and a crown was on His head as He rode forth conquering and to conquer. When He opened the second seal, a flaming red horse came out to take peace from the earth.   Men will slay one another.   A huge sword was given to Him.

The third seal sent forth a black horse and in the riders hand was scales, or balances.   A voice in the midst of the four creatures was saying, "A quart of wheat for a denarius (a days wages), three guarts of barely for a denarius, and do not harm the oil or the vine.

The forth seal sent forth a horse that was ash colored.   A forth of the earth will be destroyed by death and Hades with sword, famine, and pestilence, and wild beasts of the earth by his power and authority given him to do so.

All the angels, the twenty-four elders and the four living creatures were around the throne of God and said," Salvation to our

God who sits on the throne".

Many will try to hide from the Lord, going into caves and hiding in the rocks. They will be hiding from the deep seeded indignation of the wrath of the Lamb, Jesus Christ. At the day of His wrath, who will be able to stand?

The earth, sea and the trees will not be harmed until the bond servants of our Lord God are sealed upon their heads (the 144,000). All who do not have the mark, from the temple out into Jerusalem all shall be slain. They were rebellious and perverse and did not listen to God. Much wickedness was in Israel.

All will cry to the Lord God saying: Salvation is due to our God who is seated on the throne and before the Lamb (Jesus). All will be dressed in white robes and waving palm leaves in their hands. All will cry: Blessing, and glory, and majesty, and splendor, and thanks, and honor, and power, and might be ascribed to our God forever. Amen

Jesus will be shepherd to all in the midst of the throne, and will guide all to the river of the living waters, or the water of life, and all tears will be wiped away from their eyes. All these will have came out of the great tribulation.

During the tribulation there will be locusts given the same sting as a scorpion coming out of the bottomless pit. A large shaft was opened called an abyss. It was the bottomless pit. A star called Wormwood fell like a burning torch to the earth, and opened a shaft and smoke came out of it like a great furnace. The locusts hurt men for five months. Abaddon in Hebrew and Apollon in Greek were given the power as king over them. He was an angel that fell like a star and made the bottomless pit (The Abyss). The locusts were given in their tails a sting with power to punish men for five months. The locusts had crowns on their heads and breastplates of iron. They had long hair like a woman would have. They were not to hurt the herbs or grass.

The sixth angel sounded the trumpet and a solitary voice came from the four horns of the golden altar before God. The voice said to release the four angels that were chained up in the Euphrates. The four angels were for the hour, day, month and the year to destroy a third of mankind. There was an army of two hundred million horsemen. John heard the number of them. He saw the vision of them with riders that had breastplates of fire the color of Hyacinth and of brimstone. The horses had heads like lions, and fire, smoke and brimstone coming out of their mouths. The power of the horses was in their mouths and in their tails. Their tails were like serpent heads and they did harm with them.

The rest of mankind did not repent. After these plagues they still worshiped hand-made idols of gold, silver, bronze, stone, and wood. These could not see, hear or walk. The people were still murderess sorcerers. They were immoral, and were thieves.

There was an angel with his left foot on the sea, and with his right hand he gave John a little black book and John swallowed it. It taste like honey and was bitter in the stomach. John was to prophecy later concerning many peoples and nations, and tongues and to the kings. The temple with people worshiping was recorded by John. The others as unbelievers trampled down the outside for 42 months, which is three and one-half years.

★ **Power will be granted to the two witnesses.** The two witnesses were called the sons of oil. The two witnesses are: Joshua the High priest, and Zerubbabel the prince of Judah (the two anointed ones). They are the two lamp stands that are before the Lord of the whole Earth. A golden bowl of oil was on each lamp stand. They are also referred to as the two olive trees before the Lord God of the whole earth. Fire will come out of their mouths to consume anyone who desires to harm them.

One of the two witnesses was Zerubbabel and the Lord says, "Not by might nor, by power but, by My Spirit (of whom the oil is a symbol) says the Lord of Hosts". The oil is the oil of the olive trees (the two witnesses). These represent the Spirit of the Living Lord God. Zerubbabel and Joshua led the exiles out of Babylon and, they also built the temple. The hands of Zerubbabel laid the foundation of the temple. Authority (power) was given to Joshua the High Priest and, Zerubbabel the Prince of Judah. They are the two olive trees and the two lamp stands that stand beside the Lord God of the whole earth. If anyone desires to harm them, fire proceeds out of their mouths and devours their enemies. They have the power to shut up the sky so rain will not fall during the days of their prophesying. They will have power over the waters and will turn them into blood and, will smite the earth with every plague as often as they desire.

They will be killed by the beast that will come out of the abyss and overcome them by war. Their dead bodies will be laid in the streets of the mystically called great city called Sodom and Egypt where the Lord Jesus was also crucified. The people rejoice over their death. They will lay dead in the street for three and half days. **Then the breath of God comes into them and they stand to their feet.** Fear comes over the people. The loud voice of God comes from Heaven and says," Come up here". They will go up into Heaven in a cloud, as the people watch.

• **We give thanks, "Oh Lord God the Almighty" Who is and who was. You have taken Your power and You are reigning.** The devil was thrown out of Heaven with the bad angels. The angel Michael and his angels waged war with the devil (Satan) and threw him and his angels out of Heaven.

A loud voice in Heaven said, "Now the salvation and the power and the Kingdom of our God and the authority of His Christ have come, for the accuser of our brethren has been thrown down. The aged old serpent accused day and night before God.

A beast came up out of the sea, (The dragon). The devil gave the beast his own power, his might, and his throne and great dominion. One of his heads had a deadly wound. It was healed. The dragon went after Israel, and Israel went to the desert to retreat for three and one-half years. The earth swallowed up the waters the dragon tried to overcome them with. He then went after the saints who remained who had a testimony and believed in God and His commandments. They overcome by the blood of the Lamb and the words of their mouth. They did not love and cling to life. They died by their testimony.

The devil knows his time was short. He wants to take as many as he can with him. We must believe in Jesus Christ as our Savior and die believing in Him if we want to go to Heaven and be with Him forever. Fire and brimstone are awaiting those who do not. They will go with Satan forever into the lake of fire. The eternal gospel will have been preached to every tribe, nation, tongue, and people who lives on the earth.

The beast will deceive people into believing in him and worshiping him. He will perform miracles and signs from the sky. He will put to death those who will not bow down and worship the image of the beast. He will want to put a stamp or mark of his number on their hand or forehead. The number is 666.

Standing on Mt. Zion were the 144,000 men ransomed and redeemed from the earth. They who had the name of the Lord and the Father inscribed on their foreheads. They sang a new song before the throne of God. No one knew the song but them. They were not defiled by relations with women. They were pure as virgins. They are those who follow the Lamb wherever He goes. These are the ones who have not lied. They were Blameless, spotless, untainted, without blemish before the throne of God. They are the first fruits for God and the Lamb.

An angel cried with a mighty voice, "Revere God and give glory and honor and praise in worship!" "The hour of judgment has arrived!" Fall down before Him and pay homage and adoration and worship Him who created heaven and earth, the sea and the springs (fountains) of waters!" A cloud of smoke was present. Smoke is the Shekinah glory of God's presence. (Revelation 15)

Jesus will reap the harvest from the earth. The rest will see the wrath and indignation of God. Jesus will be sitting on a cloud as the Son of Man and will have a crown of gold upon His head. He will put in the sickle when the hour to reap the harvest comes. The harvest will be ripe. This is the rapture.

An angel with the power of fire will put his sickle to the earth to gather the clusters from the earth and outside of the city will throw them into the winepress of the wrath of God. Blood will be seen for two hundred miles. This is in Revelation; chapters, 15, and 16.

God finishes His wrath upon the earth with seven plagues. God has power over the seven plagues and the great earthquake is the end of Babylon the Great and is given a cup of the wine of the fierce wrath of God.

The great day of the almighty will bring demons performing signs, frogs with unclean spirits from the false prophet, the beast and the dragon's mouth. They will gather for war against the Lord with the kings of the whole world. This is the great day of God.

He says," Behold I come like a thief in the night." "Blessed is the one who stays awake and is clothed in righteousness." This gathering will be called the, Har-mageddon in Hebrew / Arma-geddon in another dialect. God will give power to the angels to employ each of seven plagues during the tribulation. People who are unbelievers, the ones who go to a church and do not follow the truth of the Lord, who are in a backslidden state of being, (people that have blasphemed, and are unrepentant) and those who do not believe Jesus is the Messiah come and is coming again, will be in the tribulation. This is in Revelation; chapters, 16, and 17.

The seven plagues will come upon the earth by the power of God. The plagues will come upon anyone who has the mark of the beast, will not repent or give the Lord God glory. They will blaspheme God even though fierce heat is scorching them. There are seven kings on seven mountains, as heads of nations and one is Jerusalem, where the woman sits. The beast is the eighth king. There were ten kings who have not been a king. These kings are the ten horns, and are kings with the beast for one hour.

Hallelujah! Salvation and glory and power belong to our God and Jesus Christ. He is King of Kings and Lord of Lord's. We will rejoice and be glad, and give glory to Him for the Marriage Supper of the Lamb will come and His bride will make herself ready, dressed in robes of righteousness, and dressed in white pure clean linen. Fine linen represents the righteous acts of the saints. This refers to all who overcome the world by the precious blood of the Lamb, or the Lord Jesus Christ. Blessed are those who are invited to the Marriage Supper of the Lamb, Jesus Christ our King and Our Father God of heaven and the New Jerusalem to come down and set under a New Heaven and, a New Earth.

The POWER of GOD
SCRIPTURE REFERENCES

New American Standard: Ex 15:6; Jdg 7:2; Deut 8:18; 9:29; 1 Chr 29:11; Job 40:16; Ps 49:15; Pro 3:27; Is 40:29; Jer 18:21; Mt 6:13; Mk 5:30; 9:1; 13:26; 14:62

Lk 1:35; 4:14; 22:6; Act 8:10; 17:8; Ro 1:4, 16; 15:5; 1 Co 1:18, 24; 2:4-5; 15:4, 56; 2 Co 12:9; 13:14; Eph 1:21; Heb 1:3; 11:34; 1 Pe 3:22

Amplified: Gen 32:28, 30; 31:6, 29; 33:20; 49:3; Ex 15:6; Deut 8:18; 9:29; 32:36; 1 Chr 29:11; Ezr 8:22; Job 26:2, 24; 36:5; 37:23; 40:16; Ps 29:4; 33:16; 62:10-12; 63:2, 6; 66:3; 84:7; 89:13-14, 42; 93:1; 110:3; 145:11; Pro 3:27; 18:21; Eccl 6:4; 8:8;

Is 40:29; Jer 10:12; 15:15; Hos 12:3; Mi 3:8; Na 1:3; Hab 1:11; 3:4; Zec 4:6

Mt 9:8, 22:29; 28:18; Mk 5:30; 9:1; Lk 1:35; 4:14; 5:17; 6:19; 22:53, 65; 24:49; Jo 1:12; 2:11; 10:18; 16:33; 17:2; 19:10-11

Act 18:28; 26:18; Ro 1:4; 1:16; 1:20; 6:9; 9:22; 15:5; 1 Co 1:8, 24, 26, 28, 35; 2:4; 4:20; 5:4; 6:12; 15:43, 56; 2 Co 4:7; 12:9-10; Eph 1:19, 21; 6:12; Php 3:10; Col 1:11; 2:10, 15

2 Thess 1:9; 1 Ti 6:16; 2 Ti 1:7; 3:5; Heb 1:3; 2:4, 14: 4:12; 6:5; Ja 1:21; 1 Pe 1:3-5; Ju 1:25; Rev 2:26; 3:8; 5:13; 7:12; 113, 17; 12:10; 19:1

King James Version: Ge 32:28; 49:3; Deut 8:17-18, 32, 36; 2 Sa 22:33; 1 Chr 29:11; Ezr 8:22; Job 26:2; 26:14; Ps 62:11; Pro 3:27; 18:21; Eccl 8:4; 8:8; Is 40:29; Jer 10:12; 15:15; Hos 12:3; Mic 3:8; Hab 1:11; 3:4; Zec 4:6; Mt 9:6, 8; 22:29; 28:18; Mk 9:1; Lk 1:4, 6; 4:6; 5:17; 22:53, 69; 24:47, 49; Jo 1:12; 10:18; 16:33; 17:2; 19:10-11; Act 26:18; Ro 1:6, 20; 9:22; 13:1; 1 Co 2:7; 13:10; Eph 1:9; 2:2; 6:12; Php 3:10; Col 1:11, 13, 16; 2:10; 2 Thess 1:9; 1 Ti 6:16; 2 Ti 1:7; 3:5; Heb 1:3; 2:14; 6:5; 1 Pe 1:5; 2 Pe 1:3; Ju 1:25; Rev 12:26; 4:11; 5:13; 7:12; 11:3, 17; 12:10; 16:9; 19:1

Notes...

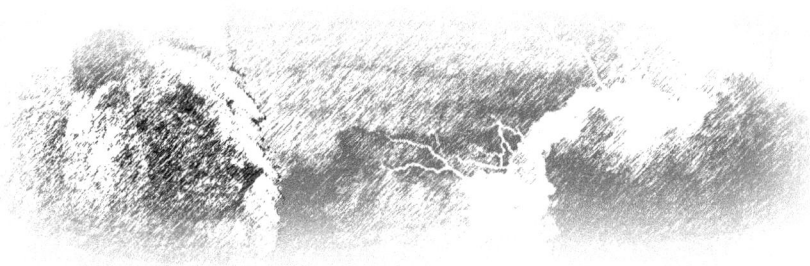

The STRENGTH of GOD

God will give Us His Strength to Live

The beginning of strength comes from the firstfruits of man's vigor and strength in his ability to achieve the assigned abilities to carry out his tasks in life according to The Word of God unto righteous living. The Lord is our strength and our song and has become our salvation. Loving God helps us carry out the abilities He has given to us to be able to achieve His greatness in us. We inherit all Jesus Christ has done. This gives us the authority to achieve the good works He assigns to us. Through Christ Jesus we can walk out the good works He has given to us with His strength and His authority. All good works are in Jesus Christ. We receive the strength that does not fail God. By God's strength in Moses, Israel was brought out of Egypt.

Because Israel did not listen and obey God, all their work did not produce increase. As they worked there land, there was no rain, no yielding fruit, and no blessing came from God. No answers came to them. Their strength was spent in vain. They were not humble, but prideful in their own power, and did not prevail.

★ **God is our strength, rest and security.** There is none like our God "O" Jeshurun (Israel). He rides through the heavens to help in His majestic glory, in the skies. In our own strength we cannot bring into light the wonderful works of our Lord God. His works are perfect.

The Rock is Jesus, and our strength. Resting in God's strength will not fail us. Our arms and hands are made strong and active by the hands of the Almighty God of Jacob (Who wrestled with the angel of the Lord and won) by the name of the shepherd, (Jesus) the Rock of Israel.

By the strength of the mighty hand of God, Israel was brought out of bondage, and from bondmen. Unleavened bread is the symbol of their deliverance. It was in the month of Abib. God triumphed over the Pharaoh and the Egyptians, as the water drowned their army after Israel went across the Red Sea on dry land. The Lord was their strength and their song and was their salvation.

Israel went into the land of milk and honey after forty years roaming the Sinai Desert because of their rebellion and idolatry.

★ God is God, and is to be praised and exalted. The Lord is a man of war. The Lord God, Almighty is His Name. Our Lord God's right hand is glorious in power. His right hand shatters the enemy by His great strength. When the enemy rises against us, You send Your fury. By the greatness of God's majesty our enemies are overthrown. The Lord will reign forever and ever and is awesome in power.

▶ **If we are not listening and obedient to the Lord, chastening and discipline will break us and show pride instead of humility.** Our power should be the power in God's strength from our inner-being. Jesus and the Father are our strength and power to ride over all that would exalt itself against us. If this happens we will fall into condemnation. All was finished by Jesus death on the cross. We are freed from our sins forever in Christ Jesus. Israel did not heed the commandments and statutes of the Lord God. Idolatry is anything that exalts itself more highly than our Lord God.

The Lord God was and is our Strength, rest and security forever. He rides through the heavens as our help and is majestic in the skies. He is our refuge and defense and is our support. He destroys our enemies as we put our trust in Him with our life. We have eternal life in Him.

★ **God is our sword and our shield** as He was for Israel even in their rebellion. He reached out to them and they would not receive Him as people saved by the Lord God with His sword and His shield. **With signs and wonders they were delivered from the bondage of Egypt.** By their own strength they could not deliver themselves.

• **He will guide the feet of the Godly.** By his own strength no man will prevail. Only by the Spirit of God will we prevail in a greater way. God is the man of strength for Israel and He will not lie or change His mind. It shall run the course as His set decision.

Seek the Lord and His strength. Yearn for and seek His face. Yearn to be in His presence continually. Remember God's marvelous deeds, miracles, and judgments He uttered in Egypt. On a holy day they ate and drank, and shared with others, and the joy of the Lord was their strength and, stronghold or shelter.

The kindness of the Almighty was the strength and endurance given to Job during adversity. God is wise in heart and mighty in strength. We cannot harden our hearts against Him, and expect to be safe and prosper in our ways. We should be as He is in our hearts also. God has all the answers to all our questions. He is the wisdom and the knowledge we need to live and be safe and prosperous in our lives while we live here on this earth.

★ **God is strength and justice.** We need not to ask Him for either one. He is our all in all. God is our life, strength, and justice in all things. We will love the Lord fervently, and be devoted to Him for He is our strength. **The Lord is our Rock, our fortress, and our deliverer:** Our God is keen and firm in strength and in Him will we will trust and take refuge. He is our shield, and the horn of our salvation.

★ **God is our high tower.** We call upon the Lord Our God, and He hears us from His Holy Heaven. He is worthy of our praise and will save us from our enemies. Our enemies can be anything or anyone that will cause us to stumble or lose our strength, and not be able to stand in adversity, and not live in the victory of the cross.

God guards us with His strength, and makes our way perfect in Him. He is our shield and refuge and we should trust in Him. **God is our Rock. There is none beside Him in whom we can trust.** He is God and girds us with strength, and makes our way perfect.

When we are able to walk like hind's (deer) feet in progress, and testing, and trouble, He sets us securely upon our highs places. Our feet will not slip. We can fight any battle girded with the strength of the Lord our God. **He puts our enemies under our feet and they bow down and cannot rise up against us. Those who hate us will turn their backs. He holds us up.** He listens to us and does not listen to our enemies. We call Him and our enemies cannot overtake us. We have His strength and His deliverance, and have His salvation. The Lord is our strength and our impenetrable shield. Our hearts will greatly rejoice, and with our songs we will praise Him always. He is our unyielding strength. He is our stronghold of salvation. We are His anointed. We are His people and, He will bless us as His inheritance. He will nourish, and shepherd us, and carry us forever. Jesus is our Shepherd, and our everlasting salvation. The Lord sat as King over the deluge. The Lord still sits as King forever.

• **The Lord will give unyielding, and impenetrable strength to His people.** The Lord will bless His people with peace. The Lord looks over the entire inhabitation of the earth. He knows our hearts, and our doings. No king or his great army can be delivered or a mighty man delivered by his own strength.

It is God who keeps us alive in war or, famine or death. **He is the author and finisher of our salvation.** When the righteous cry for help, the Lord hears and delivers us from all our distresses, and troubles. The Lord is close to those who are of a broken heart and saves such as are crushed with sorrow for sin, and are humbled and have a repentant heart.

Many evils confront us, but **the Lord will deliver us from them all.** We are the righteousness of God in Christ Jesus. Jesus Christ His Son is of strength and salvation. Our strength fails us, but God is our strength, and deliverer from all adversity. Our enemies will not rejoice over our failures. We will prevail in the strength of the Lord our God. A prayer with cheerfulness and encouragement with strength will come to us with gladness and will always be ours as we consider the Lord as we perish from the earth.

You are the God of our strength and will deliver us from the stronghold of deceitful and unjust men. We will take refuge in You oh God! You are our strength. Your light and truth will save us from our enemies. God is our exceeding joy, and we will praise Him continually.

You are King O God! You are the victory and the deliverer as You were for Jacob (Israel). Our enemies are pushed down, and we tread on them who rise up against us. We will trust in the light and truth of the Lord our God's strength, and salvation leading us to deliverance from our enemies. Wisdom and truth are in the inner-man. This is the desire of God for us to know wisdom in our inmost heart.

★ **God is our refuge and strength, mighty and impenetrable to temptation.** And is a very present and well-proved help in the time of trouble. We should sing praise to our God. He is our strength. Sing praise to Him, He is our defense, and our high tower. Our God shows mercy and steadfast love to us in the day of our distresses. We should sing of His mighty strength and power. We should sing aloud of His mercy and His grace and His loving kindnesses toward us in the morning. He is our Rock (Jesus Christ) of unyielding strength and our refuge is in God.

God is awe-inspiring, profoundly impressive, and is terrible out of His high places. Blessed be our God. Ascribe power and strength to our God. His majesty is over Israel and His strength and might are in the skies. Be with us O Lord! when our strength and power fail us. We will praise and honor our Lord God all the day long. We will receive strength to do the mighty acts of God. Our flesh may fail and our heart may fail, but the Lord our God is the Rock and firm strength of our hearts, and our portion forever.

▶ **Sing a-loud, shout for joy to our Lord God our strength.** He is the Lord God of Jacob (Israel) the Church. We are all God's children. Blessed, happy, and fortunate, and to be envied, is the man whose strength is in You, O Lord our God. Your heart and our hearts are in the highways of Zion, The Church. The blessed of the Lord go from strength to strength increasing in victorious power. Each appears before God in Zion (Church). We will spend our days in the courts of the Lord, which is better than a thousand anywhere else.

The STRENGTH of GOD

God, how lovely are Your tabernacles (us). Our hearts and our soul should yearn and get homesick for the courts of the Lord our God. Our flesh and our heart should cry out and sing for joy to our Living God. Our strength comes from the strength we have in the gathering of the saints (us) in the worship of God in the congregation of The Church. There we will find the highways of the Lord God of Zion (The Church). We will look by the Spirit of the Lord upon the face of Jesus our shield as the anointed in the congregation of Zion (The Church). No good thing, will God withhold from those who walk upright. Even the sparrow and the swallow nest in His altar. O Lord of Hosts, my King and my God, You are to be praised, worshiped and adored in the congregation of the anointed ones who are the righteousness of God in Christ Jesus.

We are blessed, happy, fortunate and to be envied because we have You Lord God as our King, and Your strength in us forever. In You are the High ways of Zion (The Church), Jerusalem. In dry places we receive a place of springs of rain water as blessings to us from You O Lord our God and King. The Jew and the Gentiles will be blessed as the church of our most Holy Lord God and King, Jesus Christ. The Lord is our strength and our redeemer. We go from strength to strength increasing in the victorious power of the Lord our God. We receive blessings as we are in Zion (The Church) Jerusalem. The blessings come from the Lord God our King.

When we are tempted, the Lord our God will grant us strength and flexibility in power to resist temptation by His mercy and gracious loving-kindness. He is slow to anger in His loving-kindness toward us in mercy and grace. All others will see Your goodwill and approval toward us by Your goodwill and favor toward us will as a sign of evidence to them. Their hate and shame will not matter to us. We only care that You forgive, help and comfort us.

Those who hate us will be put to shame by You O Lord our God and King. You are our help and comforter. You are the glory of our strength as our proud adornment and by Your favor as our Horn exalted, and we walk with uplifted faces. The Lord is our strength and our shield. He is the Holy One of Israel.

God endowed Jesus Christ His Son Who is mighty (a hero) giving Him the power to help as Champion of Israel. He, Jesus Christ is exalted the Chosen from among the people of Israel. He, Jesus Christ is God greatly feared and revered in the council of holy angelic ones. He is to be fearfully; worship-fully revered above all those who are around about Him. His faithfulness is around about Him as an essential part of Him always. His throne to all generations is mercy and loving–kindness. He is the seed established forever, unchangeable and perpetual. The world is established and cannot be moved.

★ **The Lord reigns; clothed in majesty.** He as Lord is robed and has girded Himself with strength and power. Honor and majesty are before Him. Strength and beauty are in His sanctuary. Ascribe to the Lord; O' you families of the peoples, ascribe to the Lord; glory and strength. He will weaken our strength to humble us before Himself in glory and reverence. He has come to set the captive free. We will reign with Him forever in His strength.

The Lord will send forth from Zion (The Church) Jerusalem the scepter of His strength. We are the power in Jesus, and we will ourselves willfully in the day of His power in the face of our enemies, be His glory, honor, and majesty. We are to be dressed in the beauty of holiness and in the holy array of Jesus the womb of the morning. He will be triumphant in us. The Lord is our strength and our song and has become our salvation. The righteous right hand of the Lord God does valiantly, and achieves strength through us.

As we are tempted to do something that is not good for us, we call and the Lord our God answers us and strengthens us with strength by might, and flexibility in our inner-man that will not lead us into temptation to do evil, or make wrong choices. In the time of battle, God covers our head with the strength of His salvation. Surely the uncompromisingly righteous shall give thanks to Your name O Lord God. The upright shall dwell in Your presence before Your very face. Blessed is the Lord our Rock, and keen and firm strength. He teaches our hands to war and our fingers to fight. We are the army of God in Jesus Christ His Son. God does not delight in the strength of a horse, nor does He take pleasure in the legs of a man's strength. The Lord takes pleasure in those who reverently and worshipfully fear Him (God). We are those who have hope in His mercy and His loving-kindness.

O' Jerusalem! Praise Your God, O' Zion (The Church)..... He is to be exalted, to be praised and is to be honored by all who are His people. The ones called by His name. We are Christians called by His name which is above all names. Jesus Christ is our one God and King of all kings. He is Lord of all.

▶ **We are to praise and sing to the Lord, in the assembly of His saints.** We are His saints who believe in the Lord Jesus Christ. We are to sing in choirs or chorus, and dance in single or as a group. Israel rejoices in Him their maker. May the children of Zion (The Church) triumph, and be joyful in Him, the Lord God our King. He takes pleasure in His people. He beautifies the humble with salvation though wretched they have victory in Him.

He has strengthened, and protected, and blessed the children of God within the gates of Jerusalem and Zion (The Church). The glory of young men is their strength, and the beauty of old men is their gray hair, suggesting wisdom, and experience. From the innermost parts of a man God will arise, glory, strength, wisdom, and experience for any endeavor called upon in its time. If you faint during adversity your strength is small, or you are weak. God will not give His strength to loose women, or someone who wants to ruin or, destroy a King. If a man is lacking in strength in a day of distresses, he will be limited in strength for whatever he has to have strength of heart to do, or go through. Young men do not give your strength to loose women. These loose women ruin and destroy kings. Anyone in high esteem will be brought low in stature by the loss of their strength in the Lord.

Use wisdom to acquire more strength, and salvation as our song. He has become our salvation. Judah should have been mindful of the Rock as their strength, and their stronghold, and not idols. They were doing things (bowing) to idols, in their own strength, to Adonis a strange god. Their flowers withered and their plantings failed to grow.

Ships of Tarshish will have no coast in Tyre, for their strength. Israel will not burn if they make peace with God and rely on His protection. The Lord God The Holy One of Israel said: *If you return to Me, and repent and rest in Me, I will be your strength, and you shall be saved; in quietness and in (trusting) confidence I shall be your strength.* Israel, would not.

- **God gives strength to the weary and to the one who is lacking in might, He will increase His power to him.** We are to expect and look for our hope in the Lord. To do this is to renew our strength, and see changes that will empower us. We shall lift up our wings and mount up (close to God) as eagles (mount up to the sun): **We shall run and not be weary; we shall walk and not faint,** and become tired.

- **We should look away from things that would distract us from Jesus.** This way we will not grow weary and exhausted, lose heart, relax and faint in our minds. Jesus is the leader, source of our faith, bringing us toward perfection. He endured the cross and is seated at the right hand of the Father God. He endured every encumbrance (unnecessary weight) the sin which so cleverly entangles us. He endured the cross so we can obtain the prize of the joy of no shame as we reach maturity with Him. We can run and finish the race for the highest calling of God in Christ Jesus. He is the author and finisher of our faith.

Only in the Lord, can we say that we have righteousness and salvation, victory and strength to achieve. All who are against Him will be ashamed. Jesus Christ is by The Holy Spirit alive in us as: We are the temple of the Holy Ghost.

In the Lord, all Israel will be justified; enjoy righteousness, salvation and victory and they shall glory. When we are weakened in strength as we labor, our labors will not be in vain in the Lord. Our recompense is with our God. He formed us from the womb. We are honorable in the eyes of the Lord our God, and He has become our strength. God's salvation extends to the ends of the earth.

Jeremiah said, "Lord, You are my stronghold". "The nations will know that You are the Lord". The nations will see the power and the strength of the Lord our God. In days of our afflictions as they were to Jeremiah, God will be our strength and stronghold. God will be our refuge. There is no profit without the things of God.

The nations will be made to know by His power and His strength (might) that His Name is the Lord. The nations will come from the ends of the earth. Therefore; the Lord says, I will make the nations know this one time, that it is My power and strength, and by My might they will know that My name is the Lord God almighty. The Lord God profaned His sanctuary because Israel was taking pride in their own strength. The Lord God is the sovereign ruler. He calls forth obedience and loyalty in His presence. God took their temple away, which was their strength and stronghold. God wanted to heal Israel, and none among them would call on God their Lord.

Ephraim (the ten northern tribes) went from country to country to find favor and strangers devoured their strength, and they did not know it. Israel testifies against Ephraim, and they do not return to the Lord their God, and did not seek or inquire of Him in spite of all they did. Ephraim was weak, without heart, or understanding. Israel calls to Egypt and they go to Assyria. Woe to them, they have wandered away from Me; says the Lord their God. Destruction will come to them because of their rebellion, and trespasses. The Lord would have redeemed them. They spoke lies against the Lord, God. They were idolatrous people.

Jacob became strong, and contended, and had power with God. Jacob's name was called Israel because he wrestled with the Angel of the Lord, and won at a place called Bethel in the land of Luz. Jacob took His brother, Esau's birthright by deceiving Isaac, their father. Jacob held on to Esau's heel when they were born. God saw the strength of Jacob at birth. Esau, become a skillful hunter. Jacob was a peaceful man living in tents.

Though the fig tree does not blossom, and there is no fruit on the vines, though there's no product of the olive trees, and the fields yield no food and though the flock is cut off from the fold, and there is no cattle in the stalls, yet will I rejoice in the Lord, I will joy in the God of my salvation, the Lord my God is my strength. We will exult in our victorious Lord our God.

The Lord said; return to Me, hold fast to love and mercy, and righteousness and justice, and wait expectantly for your God continually. The Lord is our strength, and our personal bravery and our invincible army. He makes our feet like hind's (deer) feet, and makes us walk and make spiritual progress in our walk, so we will stand in the time of terror in our high places of trouble, suffering, or responsibility. He Who is Almighty has done great things for us, and holy is His Name [to be venerated (respected and revered) in His purity, majesty, and glory]. We are to humble ourselves in the presence of the Lord our God.

He has mercy, kindness and compassion for those who are afflicted and miserable. We should fear Him with godly reverence from generation to generation, and age to age. He has shown strength and might with His arm. He has scattered the ones who are proud and haughty by the designs of their hearts.

Be alert and on your guard; stand firm in your faith, (your conviction respecting man's relationship to God, and Divine things). Keep trust and holy fervor, born of faith and a part of it.

• **Act like men and be courageous; grow in strength**. Let everything you do be done in true love to God, and man as inspired by God's love for us as His children. The Lord says; My grace (unmerited favor) and loving-kindness and mercy is enough for you (sufficient against any danger, and enables you to bear the trouble manfully). My strength and power are made perfect (fulfilled and completed) and show themselves most effective in your weakness. In our weaknesses and infirmities, the strength and the power of Christ Jesus our Messiah does rest, pitch a tent and dwells over us.

• **Each of us has received a particular spiritual talent as a gift (a gracious Divine endowment) to use for one another as a benefit**. We are to be good trustees of God's many ways of grace, and be faithful stewards of the extremely diverse powers, and gifts granted to us as Christians by God's unmerited favor (grace). Whoever speaks [may he do it as one who utters], Oracles, wonders and miracles of God; who renders service. May he do it in the strength God furnishes abundantly, so that in all things, God may be glorified through Jesus Christ (the Messiah). To Him be the glory, and dominion forever and ever (through endless ages). Amen (so be it).

There are those who by the help of faith subdued kingdoms, administered justice, obtained promised blessings, closed the mouths of lions (Daniel in the lions den). They extinguished the raging fiery furnace (Shadrach, Meshach and Abednego). Others escaped the devouring of the sword, out of frailty and weakness won strength and became stalwart (Mighty and resistless in battle). They routed (defeated) alien hosts.

▶ **If we trust in the Lord, He will deliver us out of our troubles.** We should always delight in the Lord. The Lord will sustain us, refresh us, and strengthen us on our beds as we are languishing: on our bed the Lord will turn, change, and transform us in our illness.

Wine is to gladden our heart, and will make our face shine more than oil. Bread is to strengthen and support us, refresh us and, strengthen our hearts. To me this is like the relationship we have with Jesus Christ.

In the day we will call, and You will answer, and strengthen us with Your strength and might and inflexibility to temptation in our innerself. You are to be exalted, magnified in Your truth, and faithfulness.

★ **Your Name and Your Word lead us to worship You.** You Israel; My servant Jacob, whom I have chosen, descendent of Abraham; My friend. You Israel, whom I have taken from the ends of the earth, and called from the remotest parts of the earth, I have not rejected. I have chosen you Israel. Do not fear for I Am with you. Do not anxiously look around you. I will surely help you, and uphold you with my righteous right hand. I will strengthen you, and harden you during difficulties. All those who are angry will be ashamed, and dishonored. All those who contend with you will be as nothing, and they will parish.

Your maker is your Husband, the Lord of Hosts is His name --- --- and the Holy One of Israel is your Redeemer. He is called Jesus Christ the Son of God, and He is the God of the whole earth. The children of God are Jesus Christ's inheritance given Him by the Father God for His great sacrifice as **He died on the cross for all to be delivered from sin and damnation.** Salvation is our song to sing for all that our Father God, the Holy Spirit, and King Jesus Christ have done for us on Calvary.

Notes...

FAITH

A renewed mind focused on Jesus Christ

God the Father wants all of His children to believe, love, and to be faithful to Him. Do not let pride be in your soul. Be righteous, do not compromise. Live a faithful life, and live in faithfulness. The Gospel is the righteousness that God says, comes from faith which causes more faith. He says a man who lives by faith is just and upright.

Do not hinder the truth by making it inoperative, living in wrong ways. Live Godly and in righteousness before men. Love, and honor and obey God in faithfulness. Always be thankful for all He has provided for you to live a good life.

• **We are to fill the Earth with the glory of God through Jesus Christ His Son.** He will clothe us with righteousness. We will live by faith in Him, so we will not be tossed to and fro by every wind of doctrine. (These are belief patterns not of The Word of God).

• **He wants us to steadfastly follow the example of Jesus.** We are to be conformed into His character. We will find peace, and calm in the storms of life as we walk in our faith in Him. Our sins are forgiven because of our faith in Jesus Christ, and Who He is in our life.

▶ **We are healed and raised up by our faith as we take courage, and we are restored to health.** By our faith, Jesus reached out His Holy Hand to us and has saved us. He will catch us so we will not fall when we have faith in Who He is, and what He can do. If our faith is great, Jesus will do as we wish for Him to help. **We can move unwanted obstacles, circumstances, and troubles if we truly rely on, and trust in the Lord. We must believe, and not doubt having confidence in what God can do through us in Jesus Christ His Son.**

If we have faith as small as a mustard seed we can heal someone with epilepsy by praying, and fasting: Jesus told the disciples this. We must have faith by firmly relying on, and trusting in the Lord Jesus Christ. We cannot be timid or fearful stepping out into the moves of God in us. We can rebuke the winds, and calm the storms of life into perfect peace. We are a believing generation with faith in Who Jesus Christ is in us.

● **We must have confidence in Jesus that our sins are forgiven.** Our faith must be great to show forth the Glory of God in us as we follow Jesus' example. He healed a person that had been ill because of the great faith of another. The person healed was not present. We must have faith in Jesus. We must have faith in His veracity, His power, and His integrity. We need to reverence Him by not being afraid of what He can control in our lives. The Lord wants us to have untroubled, undisturbed well-being. This is peace as we walk with Him. We must believe that whoever we pray for will be made well. Having faith and confidence in the Lord, knowing what He can do through us without fear will heal others.

Fear is lack of faith and confidence in Who Jesus is in us. We must hear the Word of the Lord God, obey it and practice it. Our faith, trust, and confidence in God is; recognizing Who He is in our life, and giving thanks. Praise will spring forth from our belief in

God and restore our health. The Lord wants there to be persistence in faith on Earth when He comes. By our faith we are to pray for our brothers, and sisters to be strengthened and established in Jesus Christ. His Name through and by faith will give perfect soundness of body. We will be made well and strong before all men.

★ **He lives in our hearts, and saves our souls.** We are to be of good character, and full of the Holy Spirit with wisdom. We are to be Steadfast in prayer, and in the ministry of The Word. We are priests to God, obedient to the faith in Jesus Christ our Messiah. We have obtained eternal salvation in the Kingdom of God.

We can work great signs, and wonders among people as Stephen did with the strength, and faithful ability of the Lord. We are to be good people, full of, and controlled by the Holy Spirit. We are to live like this for the good advantage of other people. We are to be examples of the character of Jesus, so others will accept the faith. We are to be able to see by the Spirit of Truth if a person has the faith to be healed.

We are to be cleansed in our heart by our faith, (a strong welcomed conviction that Jesus is the Messiah through whom we have obtained eternal salvation in The Kingdom of God.) This is guaranteed, therefore we are to make strong (firm in the faith) churches continually. Faith in Jesus Christ is due Him for all He did for us on the Cross of Calvary. We are to be consecrated, and purified by faith in Jesus Christ.

● **Our faith in Jesus should be of good report to the World, and everywhere.** We should always have a thankful attitude toward our Lord God in Christ Jesus. We are to be mutually strengthened, encouraged, and comforted by each other's faith, yours and mine.

The Gospel of righteousness springs forth as faith leading us to fruitfulness in what The Gospel teaches us. We are to be a happy people making changes in our behavior, and living a life that is in His favor. Happiness is the Lord in our life. Faith is revealed by The Gospel of righteousness (right standing with God) Jesus in us, the hope of glory. These things bring faith to our walk. Our faith arises as we read, and believe what is written in The Gospel. Believing springs forth in faith, and the way of faith arouses more faith, increasing our faith. When we believe what is written in The Gospel, The Word of God, through faith we are justified, and righteous, and live by faith.

We are to recognize sin and work toward repentive faith, and holy character. We should not be controlled by the power of sin but, by repentance. This makes us justified by faith in what Jesus did for us as He died on the cross: He made us free from condemnation, damnation, and elimination. We are in right standing with God when we are quick to repent of our sins. We are justified and forgiven by our faith and faithfulness through Jesus Christ (our sacrifice for our sins) forever.

If we have the faith in Jesus, we are accepted as righteous, and justified by Himself, Who is righteous. We are the righteousness of God through Jesus Christ, Who is now our Savior and King forever. We should have a firm relying faith in Who Jesus is in our life. Jesus came to fulfill the law, now we live by grace in God's favor. In repentance we are justified by faith. This comes by what Jesus did for us on the cross of Calvary.

God credits a faith that is righteous; making us blessed, and happy to be envied. This is because our sins are forgiven, and they are covered by Jesus Christ's death, and resurrection. The Lord takes no account of our sins, nor holds our sins against us. We trust, and believe in Him who also justifies. It is our faith credited to us as righteousness (standing acceptable to God).

★ **Jesus Christ the Son of God.** In the Old Testament these things applied to David, then Abraham. How much more to us who believe now? A man is justified, and upright because of what Jesus Christ did for him on the Cross. This apart from the law of works or, deeds (works of the law). All this is the principle of faith, (A firm relying faith in Jesus Christ). When we have faith it is credited to us as being the righteousness of God through Christ Jesus.

Concerning the righteousness of faith; inheriting all the promise is the outcome of faith. The outcome of faith depends on our faith in Christ Jesus, that we may live by grace as stable Believers. God guaranteed this outcome because we are now, by faith Abraham's descendants. Faith was credited to Abraham as he listened to God, and went to sacrifice his son Isaac before God. God supplied the sacrifice of a lamb in the place of Isaac. **Our sacrificial Lamb is Jesus.**

We are brought into the covenant by faith giving God glory and praise, by faith. God's will is to do what He is able to do, and do mightily what He has promised now. If we believe what the Lord can do, by faith it is credited to us as righteousness. (We have right standing with God).

• **We believe that Jesus Christ was raised from the dead.** This makes us acceptable to God. Jesus secured our justification, to be saved from our sins. He absolved us our guilt before God. We are forgiven forever by His grace being sufficient for us. Our account is paid in full. We are acquitted. We cannot be tried again. Righteous standing with God is credited to us acceptable to God and granted to us as believers. We trust in, and cling to and rely on God Who raised Jesus our Savior from the dead, (His Only Begotten Son). We are saved by Faith in what Jesus did for us on the cross, strengthening us when we are weak. We are justified, forgiven, and are in good health when we have faith. We can firmly stand before God in the state of favor, and grace. We rejoice, and exalt, enjoying our experience of the Glory of God.

We should depend on faith, **not in what we can do, but what Jesus has done.** We will not stumble because Jesus is the Cornerstone. He helps us up by His Holy Hand. We will not be ashamed if we trust and rely on Jesus. The outcome of our faith is Jesus as the promised Messiah. He is our Rock, our tried Stone of offence. We are the children of God with Israel (Jews) and Gentiles (us). We are to pray for the Jews to believe that Jesus has come, and is coming again, He as our Messiah. We are all called according to His purpose. (What He did on the cross for us all). The Jews are dying by the law and are missing the grace of God, because they do not believe that Jesus died for them to acquire the grace of God on the cross. Pray they find faith, and favor in Jesus Christ in God the Father.

▶ **We need to speak out freely, confess with our heart and lips by faith that Jesus Christ is Lord.** He has raised us from the dead, and we are free, and saved from our sins. Faith came by hearing the Word that came from Jesus Christ our Messiah's lips. Faith is: believing His message by which we are redeemed from sin by salvation. Jesus became Royalty on the cross to make us a royal priesthood to the glory of God the Father.

Faith is delivering His message to all the Earth, and all the boundaries of the World. We are established by faith to do these works of salvation in Jesus' Name. As children of God we stand in awe of all that is true in Who Jesus Christ is, living in us. By faith we are by believing made into His image. We are grafted into the family of God by faith in His Son Jesus Christ. We each have a degree of faith apportioned to us by God in Jesus Christ. This is grace the unmerited favor of God the Father.

We are one body not unequally yoked in Jesus Christ, because God is no respecter of persons. All of our fruitions, and talents, and qualities differ according to the grace He has given to us each individually. For example we prophesy according to the faith apportioned to us. A servant does acts of service, and mercy with genuine cheerfulness, and joyous eagerness. By faith we show honor to one another with sincere love doing what is good, affectionately in Jesus Christ. We do all things as unto the Lord. Jesus said: when you do something to or, for one of these my little ones, (the children of God) it is as if you have done it to Me, or for Me. Jesus said: love one another.

● **We are all His little children. We are His inheritance.** He loves us all. We must be obedient to the faith to win souls for our eternal God. Jesus has betrothed us to Himself in His stability, and faithfulness and we should know Him, recognize Him, be acquainted with Him, appreciate Him, understand Him and cherish the Lord Jesus Christ. We should love the Lord God Almighty with all our heart, our mind, with all our soul, and all our strength. We should not put any other gods before Him. He is the only God our Father, and Jesus is Lord, and Savior.

Faithfulness is the work of the Holy Spirit. *The Word says to build ourselves up in our most holy faith praying in the spirit (Unknown Tongues), our heavenly language.* Speaking in an unknown tongue and interpreting it is done by the Spirit of God. Other fruits of the Spirit are: love, joy, (gladness), peace, patience, (even temper), forbearance, kindness, goodness, generosity, gentleness, (meek, and humble), self-control, self-restraint, moderation, temperance, in all things.

We should be living wherever we are with confidence in ourselves as a child of God; Who is good always. We are not to participate, or believe in the works of dark living. We are to be lights in the darkness. We are to show those in darkness the way of light (Jesus in us). When we live this way, no one can bring a charge against us.

The winning of nations for God into eternity is to win them to be obedient to the faith. This is the command of the eternal God, Our Father in Heaven. We are to win nations to Jesus Christ Who is the Glory of God. Our faith does not rest in the wisdom of men, but by the empowerment of the Spirit of God (Jesus Christ) in us. Faith is the working of wonders in us by the power of God. Words of wisdom, words of knowledge, healings and miracles with understanding, all come to us by faith in Jesus Christ. He gives the power to us to express, and to perform extraordinary wonders of God.

We have prophetic insight, discernment of true or, false spirits. Speaking in an unknown tongue and interpreting it comes by the Spirit of God in us. This is done by acquiring faith in (Who Jesus Christ is) in us. We must have the love of God in us to work by faith and glorify God.

When we preach that Jesus Christ is (risen), our faith is of truth, and bears fruit, founded in Who He is in our life. By our faith Jesus Christ has put all our enemies beneath our feet. By faith God is in all and everything to us as our supreme in dwelling, and the controlling factor of our life. By faith we are alive in Jesus Christ, and shall not die, but be raised by Him into eternity. Be aware, watch, and stand firm in your faith. Our relationship to God, and divine things, are our faith. Everything we do in the true love of God, and to man is inspired of God's love for us.

Trust and fervor of faith are our actions of courage causing us to grow in strength. These things are functioning in our life toward the expectation of the coming of the Lord again to receive us to Himself forever. We should work together as believing laborers promoting joy, and faith that Jesus is our Messiah. By the spirit of faith we speak out what we believe about the life of Jesus for us and in us. We walk by faith regulating, conducting, and believing in our relationship to God by trust, and holy fervor. We walk not by sight, or appearance. We strive to please Him. We walk by faith respecting our relationship with God.

By faith we contribute to the work of God graciously, with the expectancy of Jesus Christ return as our faith grows. Examine, test, and evaluate yourselves, whether you are holding to your faith, showing forth the proper fruits of the work of God. We should prove ourselves. Know The Gospel so we will be strong, and perfect in our souls. If we do these things we will be made what we ought to be toward others promoting the love of God, and peace.

Paul, the Apostle of the Lord being called and set apart before he was born, reviled, persecuted, and set out to ruin and destroy the faith. The Lord came to him as a great light, and asked him why he was persecuting Him? Paul was forgiven, and he proclaimed the faith and God was glorified as the author, and source of what had taken place in him. God unveiled, disclosed, His Son Jesus in him to proclaim Jesus among the Gentiles (us). He proclaimed the glad tidings of The Gospel which was of God, not men. Paul became one of the messengers of Christ Jesus to spread The Gospel, and faith, love, truth and peace from God the Father in Christ Jesus.

We know that we are justified, and are in right standing with God. This is not, by works but, only through faith, and absolute reliance, and adherence to, and trust in Christ Jesus the (Messiah the Anointed One). We are justified by faith, not by rituals of law or, by works. Christ the Messiah lives in us, and the life we live in the body is by faith in and by adhering to, and trusting the Son of God. He loved us and gave His life up for us to be with Him forever. This is God's gracious gift to us.

We need to realize how important it is to have faith in what God did for us. This is grace (the unmerited favor of God) for us. We received the Holy Spirit by the message of faith. We live by faith in Jesus Christ living in us. We live by the consequences of faith by the promise of a Savior through Abraham, who was told, "That through him all nations of the earth will be blessed. We live by faith and are justified in right standing with God, and will live forever. As we received the promise through believing in Jesus Christ, we through faith have received the Holy Spirit. Jesus is the promise, come down through the linage of Abraham, by the Holy Spirit to the Jew's first then to the Gentile's (us). In Christ Jesus we are all Son's of God through faith.

God's people were guided by the law until Jesus came to fulfill the law by faith. The law was the trainer before the sacrifice of Jesus to fulfill the Law. Faith in Him is forgiveness for our sins once and for all. We are the offspring of Abraham's seed, Jesus Christ's heirs according to the Promise. Our hope in Christ Jesus by faith is energized and expressed and working through love. God is love. We by the Holy Spirit's help anticipate, and wait to receive blessing and good. Through faith we have received free grace (God's unmerited favor). We are saved, delivered from judgment, and we are made partakers of Christ's salvation. This was not done by ourselves or our doing, but by the striving of Christ Jesus as a gift of God.

★ **We are reborn, made new in Christ Jesus.** We are to do good works, planned beforehand by God: walking the paths that Jesus prepared for us to follow. We are to live the good life He prearranged and made ready for us to live in Him: we will be living in the (Messianic Promise). We are to live a good life in the world with God. Jesus made His permanent home in our hearts. We are to be deep rooted and founded securely in love. (God is Love). We are to be empowered and strengthened by devoted love experiencing the breadth, the length and the height of love in Jesus Christ. We are to walk worthy of the divine calling with the behavior that will credit us to be called to God's service.

FAITH

Paul called himself, a prisoner of the Lord. **We are to walk by faith not sight.** We are to walk in the grace of all Jesus did for us. We are to walk in humility, unselfishness, gentleness, and be mild with patience. We are to make allowance for each other. There is one body, one God, one Spirit, and Lord of us, one faith, and one baptism.

Gifts of God are given to us each individually in indiscriminately ways. They are Christ bestowed on men (us) leading us into His rich, and bounteous gift of His life lived in us by faith. We are covered by the shield of saving faith. This shield of saving faith stops all the fiery devices of the wicked one, Satan. We are to put on the armor of God *(Ephesians 14-17)* in Christ Jesus every-day. We are consecrated people to God our Father. We open our mouth to proclaim boldly the mystery of The Good News, The Gospel. We are the ambassadors of Jesus Christ. Pray at all times (on every occasion, in every season).

We have an incorruptible love for our Lord Jesus Christ. We are all joined by love with faith from God the Father, and the Lord Jesus Christ (The Messiah, The Anointed One). We should walk like we are the children of God in Christ Jesus everywhere we go. We should be united in Spirit, in purpose, and standing side by side with one mind, having faith in the glad tidings of The Gospel.

We are to constantly, and fearlessly show forth our confidence in the deliverance, and salvation of God. This is without being fright-ened or intimidated because of our faith in what Jesus Christ did for us on the Cross of Calvary. We are to shine like bright lights in a dark world, showing men The Word of life. We are giving sacrificial of-ferings of faith to God our Father. We share in the sacrifices of other saints now, and those past, by their blood shed for the sake of The Gospel. We are energized, and are each a creation of God filled with the power, and the desire to work for His good pleasure, and satisfac-tion, and delight in us. We are to be beacons of bright light shining out clearly in a dark world.

▶ **We are to be blameless uncontaminated children of God.**
This is all done by God, and not in our own strength, only by saving
faith. By faith we are not to discredit the Name of Jesus Christ, The
Anointed One. The righteousness we acquire is not by anything we
have done. We, by saving faith acquire right standing with God.
We are God's consecrated ones by leaning our entire human personality on Jesus with absolute trust, and confidence in His power,
wisdom, and goodness. We are to love all other people of God who
are consecrated to God. Jesus made us blameless, faultless, and ir-
reproachable in His Father's presence. This was done by His flesh
through death on the cross. These things God will do provided we
stay with, and in the faith in Jesus Christ.

We are to be well-grounded, and settled, and steadfast not shift-
ing or growing away from the inspired glad tidings of The Gospel
without restriction to everyone under Heaven. We are called ministers of the faith. We are to conduct ourselves, regulate our lives
in unity with, and conformity to Christ Jesus in our Christian walk.
We have faith in the work of God displayed by raising Jesus from
the dead. We were buried with Him, and raised with Him when we
were baptized, born again in Him.

Our Gospel work, and service to God, and Jesus our Messiah,
are energized by faith, and motivated by love. We have unwaver-
ing faith in the return of Jesus Christ. We are to be patterns to
other believers. We believe in the power of the Holy Spirit with
great conviction and absolute certainty. This is our whole personality in Him. He is alive, and true, and genuine, and lives in
us. We make sacrifices to be examples to others in The Kingdom
of God, and the lost (those that do not know Jesus Christ as their
Savior) in the world.

We are to be spreading The Good News of the faith that has strengthened us and established us to exhort, comfort, and encourage others. We are to spread The Good News by steadfast faith, and love, and kindness. We pray day and night for the perfecting of the Saints in their faith. We pray for the mending of their imperfections, and lack of faith.

We are to put on the breastplate of faith, and the helmet of the hope of salvation. The love of others is to grow exceedingly toward each other in increasing, and abundant love for one another. Not everyone has faith, and is held by it. The Word of God the message as we hear, and do, and believe is effectually at work in us is as superhuman power as we adhere to, trust in, and rely on it. We are to be true sons, and daughters walking in the faith.

We are instructed by The Word to the object, purpose, and charge, as duty, and responsibility, and obligation to love. The Word of God is instruction to us to fill our hearts with love for one another. We are to admonish, and urge each other to do these things for the sake of The Gospel, and The Kingdom of God. They are to spring forth from a pure heart, and a clear conscience, and sincere heartfelt faith.

Believing in Who Jesus is in us brings about an untarnished faith, and gives us the hope He has given to us. We cannot be partakers of arguments, and purposeless talk. We are stewards over the ministry of faith. We possess the mystery of faith as Christian truth hidden from the ungodly people. Without faith it is impossible to be satisfactory to God. It is necessary for us to believe that God exists and is a rewarder of those who earnestly and diligently seek Him out. Noah built the ark by faith, and relied on God.

We have faith, and believe in God, and we are heirs, and possessors of righteousness. The Holy Spirit distinctly declares that there will be in the latter days those who stray from the faith being swayed, and lured away by deluding, seducing spirits, and doctrines taught by demon-possessed people. **We are to walk in the realm of genuine faith, and truth.** We are to be aware of false doctrines in these areas.

Everything that God has created is good and none of it should be thrown away, or refused. All should be received with thanksgiving. Things created by God are hallowed, and consecrated, set apart as sacred by the body, and blood of Jesus Christ. We should be good worthy stewards, and instructors before other brethren. We should be good ministers of Jesus Christ. We are to be nourished ourselves in the truth, and faith as good Christians following instructions closely. We are to become spiritually fit in the faith. If we fail to provide for our relatives especially those in our own family, we do not have faith, good fruits, and are no better than an unbeliever.

● **Fight for good faith.** We are summoned to eternal life. We should have good confessions of faith before many witnesses. Faith is our absolute confidence in Jesus Christ our Savior. His power dwells in us with wisdom, and goodness of faith living in us permanently. We are to follow wholesome and sound teaching in the faith, and love in us by Christ Jesus. We are to be fit, and ready for any good work of God conformed to the will of God in thought, and deed pursuing faith, love, and peace. We should have fellowship with other Christians out of a pure heart.

When we are walking we will encounter people who are obstinate, and we are to be courteous, and gentle with them in the hope that God may grant that they repent, and come to know the truth. Maybe they will acknowledge, perceive, and recognize the truth. They may be delivered from, and come to their senses, and be freed from the captivity of the devil. They will no longer be out of God's will for their life. They will know faith.

FAITH

▶ **We are to walk out our faith,** and love by the Spirit of the Lord Jesus Christ who makes His home in us by His Spirit. We are to hold onto the wholesome and sound teaching, taught with the greatest of care adapted to the precious and excellent truth. Jesus is the truth, the life, and the way. We are not to undermine the faith of others by swerving away from the truth. This makes us a stumbling block (obstacle or, an impediment) to the truth. Be in Fellowship with others of the faith who call upon the Lord out of a pure heart. Do not quarrel, or cause strife among others: preserve love and the bond of peace among other Christians.

Let your purpose in life be faith, patience, love, and steadfastness in all. Understanding for salvation comes by faith in Christ Jesus by leaning the entire human personality on God. This is with absolute trust, and confidence in His power, wisdom, and goodness. Keep the faith toward a crown of righteousness (right standing with God). Being an Apostle is a bondservant of God stimulating, promoting the faith of God's chosen people, teaching them to accurately discern, and recognize, and be acquainted with the truth. This brings them into harmony, leading them into godliness.

Paul an Apostle of God taught others these things as a bondservant of God. He is one of our great spiritual teachers, now in Heaven with God in Christ Jesus. His work for Jesus is still leading people to know the Lord Jesus Christ as their Savior unto salvation. An Apostle is to deal sternly and severely with a brother who is teaching unsoundly, and errs in the teaching of the faith.

The identity of a Christian is: temperance, seriousness, being sensible, self-controlled, sound in the faith in love, being steadfast and patient in Christ Jesus. We are to teach what is right, and noble. We are to have love, and loyal faith toward the Lord Jesus, and toward the saints (God's consecrated people). We are set apart in God. We are to tell of our identity with Jesus, and His glory. We are to promote recognition, appreciation, and understanding with precise knowledge of every good thing that is in us by faith in Christ Jesus. **The just shall live by faith.**

He, Who promised is reliable, and faithful to His Word, and has fulfilled it in many ways by promise in Jesus Christ. We are not of those who draw back to eternal misery (perdition), being utterly destroyed. We believe in, cleave to, trust in and rely on God through Jesus Christ (The Messiah) by faith preserving our soul. Our faith is the assurance of the confirmed title deed of the things we hope for being proof of the things in reality that cannot be seen by faith as real facts that are not revealed to the senses. The Israelites did not mix the message of deliverance with faith. They did not lean their entire personality on God in absolute trust, and confidence in His power, wisdom, and goodness to those who have heard the message. They were not united in faith.

We should turn to the faith of God advancing steadily toward the completeness, and perfection that belongs to spiritual maturity in faith. There were many who died in faith, and did not see the tangible fulfillments of God's promises. Many warriors and Prophets of God with the help of faith subdued kingdoms, administered justice, obtained promised blessings, and closed the mouths of lions. Jesus was with them by their faith. Many died because they would not deny their faith in God. They knew they would be resurrected to a better life.

Jesus is the leader, and source of our faith. He is the first incentive of our belief. He is the finisher, bringing faith to its maturity, and perfection. He obtained the prize of His calling by enduring the cross. The joy of the Lord is fulfilled by our faith. Now we have the joy of the Lord, as our strength. He is now seated at the right hand of the throne of His and our Father in Heaven. We are seated with Jesus in heavenly places by the Holy Spirit.

We should not relax, growing weary in well doing for the sake of His most Holy Sacrifice for our sins forever. Keep the faith and grow and grow toward the most High Calling of God in Christ Jesus. Remember the ones who taught you the Word of God. May we live a well spent life imitating their faith in the existence of God, The Creator and Ruler of the universe.

★ **God is the provider and bestower of Eternal Salvation through Christ Jesus.** We are to lean our entire human personality on God, in absolute trust, and confidence in His power, wisdom, and goodness. Faith in Jesus Christ says: He is the same yesterday, today, and forever, through all the ages past, and to the new world to come. He will reign over all forever. Praise His Holy Name!

• **The teachers of old taught us to imitate the manner of faith they walked in before us.** We are to be assured, and understand that trial, and proving of our faith brings endurance, steadfastness, and patience. These three things in our life have full play and lead us to do a thorough work making us a people, perfectly, and fully developed (with no defects) lacking nothing. We are not to fall into temptation, we are delivered from evil.

• **If we ask God for wisdom He will give it to everyone liberally, and ungrudgingly.** We in His eyes are without reproach, or fault. We must have faith in the truth, and ask without hesitating, or doubting. Do not be double minded. We are called by our faith to the true riches as an heir of God.

We are not to be snobs in the practice of the faith of Jesus Christ our Lord of glory. God has called the poor, and the rich to be rich in the faith. We in any situation can love the Lord God in Christ Jesus by faith. We as the poor or, the rich as believers can inherit The Kingdom which He has promised to those who love Him. We are to have works, deeds in actions of obedience to back it up, otherwise our faith is dead. The human body apart from the Holy Spirit is dead (Lifeless).

▶ **A prayer of faith will heal those who are sick. Anoint them with oil in Jesus' Name. If they have committed sins they will be forgiven them.** We are the righteousness of God in Christ Jesus, and our heartfelt prayer of faith makes tremendous power available, (dynamic in its working). We are to keep our hearts in order by prayer, and the confession of our sins one to another.

We are being guarded by God's power through our faith to inherit that final salvation ready for us in the last time. Our faith is more precious than the perishable gold which is tested and purified by fire. Even though we do not see Jesus we believe in Him, and exult (raise our hands), and with expressible, and glorious triumph, leading us into heavenly joy at the same time receiving the consummation of our faith, the salvation of our soul. We are called Holy unto God in Christ Jesus. By our faith we stand, and cry, Holy! Holy! Holy! Is our Lord God Almighty! Who is, and was, and is to come. We respectfully, and gratefully Praise Him singing, or saying (Hal-leigh-lu-jah).

Our hope and faith are centered, and rest on God by Christ Jesus, Who was raised by God from the dead, and given honor, and glory. All Christians in the world are to be firm in their faith to withstand the devil with established, strong immovable determination. We all as Christians will suffer the same, as brethren in the faith. The enemy roams around seeking someone to seize, and devour. The devil is subject to us, no harm will come to us. We are the inheritance of Jesus Christ. Withstand the devil by your faith in the power of God for all of us who adhere to, and believe in, and trust in the Lord Jesus Christ. God's divine nature according to His divine promises, acquire our efforts to exercise our faith by developing our Christian energy in excellence, and intelligence in the knowledge of The Word, with diligence. This is the working of our perfection in Jesus Christ.

We can balance our life by believing in faith, that we are cleansed from sin, so we will not fall under condemnation. We are filled with the Spirit of Jesus Christ. By our faith He has made His home in us. We are to always have self-control in our speech, and our actions seeking Godliness. Brotherly affection leads into Christian love. Jesus portrayed brotherly love when He died on the cross for us.

We are to develop our calling as witnesses by strengthening ourselves in the knowledge of God. We are to be steadfast in our faith so we will not stumble, or fall. All this is done by spiritual qualities, and steadfast eagerness to abound in the work of the Lord.

We have been saved, or born-again, and we have entered into The Kingdom of God. Jesus Christ becomes our Lord and Savior by our faith. We are living epistles toward an eternal life with God in heavenly realms. A realm of heaven is here on earth as a prophetic word of knowledge. This is done by a word of wisdom, or exhortation to one, or more people. This is done by a person with Knowledge, and wisdom, being moved or impelled only by the Holy Spirit. We are vessels being used by the Spirit of God. Jesus Christ living in us as a vessel being used for God's glory.

By our faith we step out into the realm of prophecy only by the moving of the Holy Spirit. No man wrote any prophecy written in the Holy Scriptures, (The Bible). The Holy Spirit spoke through men and from God's spoken Word.

Guard your faith by the conclusion that each spirit you encounter is spoken in words that have proceeded out of the mouth of God. We have false prophets in the world. We can try the spirits by recognizing whether that person who is speaking is the home of Jesus Christ living in him, or her by their life in Him. *Greater is He who lives in us than he who lives in the world.* We have to watch for the spirit of the anti-Christ (anyone living against the Spirit of God). Our faith conquers the world. We have victory over the world because we are born of God. We know we love God when we keep His ordinances, and His commands, and are mindful of His precepts, and His teachings. He wants our life in Him not to be burdensome, oppressive, or grievous to us. He wants us to love Him as our Lord, and Savior. Jesus said: There is no love greater than a brother or friend laying down His life for another.

It is a fact that Jesus Christ is the Son of God our Father in Heaven. We are to adhere to Him, and trust in Him, rely on Him at all times. *We are to build ourselves up in our most Holy faith, praying in the Holy Spirit* (unknown tongue-heavenly language) rising higher, and higher, in the Holy Spirit.

We are to guard ourselves, and keep ourselves in the love of God. We are to expect, and wait patiently for the coming of the Lord Jesus Christ. He is coming again to receive us for eternity (eternal life with Him in His Kingdom). The Kingdom of God is within us.

We are the Kingdom of God in Jesus Christ on Earth to live forever in Him. We are to keep our faith in fearful times. We do not want to give the enemy (Satan or the Devil) any occasion to interfere in our life in the truth (Jesus Christ), life in Jesus, or the way (Jesus Christ our Lord and coming King).

Jesus has shown us the path. It is our choice to follow it. Do not miss all the blessings that are in it. He has made a way when there was no way. The Lord knows our record of what we are doing in love, and faith, and service, with patient endurance. We are to hold onto our faith to be able to standup against any satanic attacks on our life in Jesus Christ.

Everyone, whose name is written in the Book of Life of the Lamb (Jesus Christ), will fall down, worship, and adore Him. Every knee shall bow down, and every tongue shall confess that Jesus Christ is Lord, and King, in Heaven, and in the world. We are not to receive the stamp of the beast upon our forehead. Keep the faith in Jesus Christ.

We are to be steadfast Saints in patience, and endurance habitually keeping God's commandments, and our faith in Jesus Christ our Savior, and King, as the people of God. We are the Saints of God (God's consecrated (set apart) people. We are all saved from our sins, by the Holy sacrifice of His only begotten Son Jesus Christ once, and for all. We should be so thankful that we are all going to be with Jesus Christ, our Brother and our soon coming King, and forever with God our Father in the New Jerusalem (Heaven come down to Earth). By faith, and believing in all Jesus Christ has done for us to have a New Heavenly Home. We have been forgiven our sins forever in Him. Jesus is at home in our mortal bodies until the day He comes for us.

▶ **We are to pray for the Jews,** God's chosen people to believe in, and receive all Jesus has done for them, and for all of the nations in the World. We as Christians are adopted children of God, because we believe in all Jesus Christ has done for us. The Lord's desire is for all Israel to become the Christian nation He predestined them to be.

We have all sinned, and have fallen short of the glory of God, but Jesus made a way for us to become His inheritance forever with Him into all eternity. ***God so loved the World that He sent His only begotten Son, (Jesus Christ) into the World,*** and through Him we are saved because we believe in Jesus Christ. Abound in faith with thanksgiving. Faith is the substance of things hoped for, and the evidence, or knowledge of things yet to come.

SCRIPTURE REFERENCES

Pages 55-57a: Deut 14:9, 15; 32:20; Hab 2:4; Joel 2:28; Mt 6:26, 30, 33; 9:2; 14:31; 15:28; 16:8; 17:20; 21:31; 25:34; Mk 2:5; 4:40; 9:19; Lk 5:20; 7:9, 50; 8:25, 48; 12:28; 17:6, 19

Pages 57b-58: Lk 8:18; 18:42; 22:32; Act 3:16; 6:5, 7; 8:1; 11:24; 13:8; 14:9; 15:9; 16:5; 20:21; 26:18; Ro 1:8, 12, 17; 3:3, 26, 28, 30; 4:5, 12

Pages 59-60: Ro 4:13, 16, 19; 5:2; 9:32; 10:8-9, 17; 11:20

Pages 61-62b: Ro 12:3, 6; 16:26; 1 Co 1:26; 2:4-5, 24; 12:9

Pages 62c-64b: 1 Co 13:2, 13; 15:14, 17; 16:13; 2 Co 1:24; 4:13; 5:7; 8:7; 10:15; 13:5; Gal 1:23; 2:16, 20; 3:2, 6, 11, 14

Pages 64c-66a: Gal 3.22-26; 5:6; 6:10; Eph 1:15; 2:8; 4:5-6, 12-13; 16-17; 6:16, 23; Php 1:25, 27

Pages 66b-68a: Php 2:17; 3:9 Col 1:4, 23; 2:5, 12; 3:7; 1 Th 1:3, 8; 3:2-3, 10; 5:8; 2 Th 1:3-4; 3:2; 1 Ti 1:2, 4-5, 14

Pages 68b-69c: 1 Ti 2:7; 3:13; 4:1, 6; 5:8, 12; 6:12; 2 Ti 1:5, 13; 2:18, 22; 3:8, 10, 15; 4:7; Tit 1:1, 13; 3:15; Phm 1:6; Heb 4:2; 6:1, 12; 10:22-23; 11:1, 3-6, 13, 28-32, 39; 12:2; 13:7

Pages 70-71c: Ja 1:1, 3, 6; 2:1, 5, 17-18, 22, 24; 5:15

Pages 72-73c: 1 Pe 1:5, 7, 9, 21; 5:9

Pages 74-75c: 2 Pe 1:5

Pages 75d-76: 1 Jo 5:4; Ju 1:3, 20; Rev 2:13; 13:10; 14:12

Section 4

The HOLY GHOST

Jesus Christ and the Spirit of God

John the Baptist was born filled with the Holy Ghost of God. He prepared the way for Jesus to come. The Holy Ghost came appearing in the bodily form of a dove, and indwelled Jesus as John the Baptist baptized Him in the Jordan River. The Father God's Voice came from heaven, and was heard like thunder, and He said: "This is my Son in Whom I am well pleased." Jesus came up out of the water enlightened by the Holy Ghost.

Mary, betrothed to Joseph, became pregnant with Jesus, by the Holy Ghost of God. The Holy Ghost of God overshadowed Mary and gave her in her womb, Jesus the Son of God.

During the time Jesus walked here, John said to the people that One Who he is not worthy to untie His shoe would come, and baptize them not only with water, but with fire also. The fire is the Holy Ghost.

When Jesus arose (resurrected), He came back, and baptized the disciples in the upper room, and they received the Holy Ghost of Him. The disciples began speaking in unknown languages, also known as the Heavenly language, and were drunk in the Spirit of the Lord our God. Tongues of fire danced upon their heads. The fire was the Holy Ghost of God. When we receive the Holy Ghost we are healed, whole, in our spirit, body, and soul. Spiritually, mentally, and emotionally we will be healed. We must believe these things of the Lord our God so we will be good lights for Him, and the world to see, and believe.

We lose our blessings in the Lord because we are not renewing our mind. We let fear abide, and we do not believe in the power of life the Holy Ghost gives us. The Word of God is our life. God the Father, said to Jesus, "When you come back to heaven, I will send the Comforter (the Holy Ghost) to guide the people who believe in You". The Holy Ghost will bring to remembrance all You have taught them. The Lord says: to pray in the Holy Ghost, to pray without ceasing, and to pray for our infirmities always. How do we pray without ceasing? We pray in our unknown tongue also called our heavenly language.

If we do not pray in the Spirit we might miss some of the blessings God has for us while we are here on earth. **To deny the Holy Ghost is to deny the Lord.** The Holy Spirit is our communication between us and the Lord. He is always present in our mortal bodies because we have His indwelling Spirit (Holy Ghost). The Holy Ghost divides the wheat (good) from the chaff (bad) by the Spirit of the Lord. This is done by praying in the unknown tongue without ceasing. It is the Spirit of the Lord God guiding us in righteousness by our faith.

• **Praying in the Holy Ghost will cause us to go Higher, and higher in our growth in the Spirit.** We must pray without doubting. When we doubt we are saying in our heart God is not God. If we know Him as our Savior, and King, and know Him personally, we know He hears us when we pray. We are questioning His life in us when we doubt.

Jesus became The Light of the world. God said, *"This is my be-*

loved Son in whom I Am well pleased." He now lives in us. The Word says: that the Father God and His Son Jesus will make Their home in Now we are seated in heavenly places with Them. These things are by the Holy Ghost Living in us. We are now the light of the world.

When the Holy Spirit of God speaks from us, it will be without thought, or premeditation of it. The Holy Ghost will teach us what to say. We open our mouth, and He will fill it with the words God will want to speak. The Word says: out of the abundance of the heart the mouth speaks. We can know ourselves by what is in our heart, by the words that come out of our mouth. The Lord lives in our heart now. We can speak for Him, by His Holy Spirit Who lives in our hearts now. We will know whether it is the Holy Ghost, or ourselves. The Word says for us to build ourselves up by praying in the Holy Ghost. We do this by praying in our unknown tongue, or our heavenly language.

When John the Baptist spoke, He spoke by the Spirit of God. The Holy Ghost was not given yet. Jesus was not glorified yet. After Jesus came He said: out of your bellies will flow living water (the Holy Ghost). Jesus died and arose, and left gifts to men. The Holy Ghost is a gift from God.

The Spirit of Truth will come, and live in you, as your Comforter (counselor, helper, intercessor, advocate, strengthener, and stand-by) the Holy Ghost of Whom the Father will send in My Name. He will testify of Me. Jesus told the disciples these things, and these things have come to pass. The Holy Ghost came to demonstrate uprightness of heart, and right standing with God. He will convict, and convince the world of sin. He will do these things through the children of God. We will demonstrate the power of the Holy Ghost.

★ **The Holy Ghost will teach us all things, and bring to re-membrance the Words of Jesus.** Jesus breathed on the disciples and said receive the Holy Ghost. Thomas, one of Jesus' disciples, was not present at that time, and did not believe that Jesus had appeared to them. Thomas said, I will not believe until I have touched the hole in His side, and felt the nail wounds in His hands. Jesus said: blessed are those that have not seen, yet believe.

The Holy Ghost will come upon us, and will teach us all things so we can be witnesses to the Jews, and other Nations. Receiving the Holy Ghost, with the evidence of speaking in the unknown tongue is a gift from our Father God. The Holy Ghost lives in us by the Spirit of the Lord God in Christ Jesus. So we should not lie in our hearts. He knows our heart. Out of the issues of the heart the mouth speaks. The Holy Ghost overcomes the evil intents of the heart. We need to pray in the Holy Ghost (unknown tongue) that builds us up to overcome evil desires, and evil intentions of the heart.

Let the Holy Ghost live in you, and build you up into the likeness (heart, and appearance) of the Lord Jesus Christ. The Holy Ghost keeps us joyful, and happy, and our countenance will cause us to shine like the stars. Follow the prompting of the Holy Spirit unto a resurrected life. Simple prompting brings results as we are obedient, and are spiritually directed. Listening from the heart filled with the love of God is the Holy Spirit in us alive, and well.

The Holy Ghost will be given to those who will obey Him and be witnesses that Jesus Christ is Prince, and Savior, and will give repentance to Israel, and will forgive them their sins. We need to obey God, and not men. We need to know the things God wants us to be obedient in.

The Holy Ghost is the Comforter sent to us by Jesus from our Father God (the Spirit of Truth) and will bring to remembrance all that Jesus has done, and Who He is. We are to be witnesses for who Jesus is, and what He has done, and is doing for us as Prince of Peace, and Savior. He is now seated at the right hand of His Father, and our Father God.   Jesus is high and lifted up because He died for our sins, and arose, and is now seated at the right hand of God our Father giving us redemption, guiding us by the Holy Ghost of God the Father in Heaven. Jesus is living in us as the Holy Ghost to witness about all He has done for us.

●**Do not resist the Holy Ghost of God.** Receive the Holy Ghost. He is a Gift from God our Father by Christ Jesus. Be not just baptized in the Name of the Lord Jesus Christ. We need to receive the baptism of the Holy Ghost also. He is the fire John the Baptist told us about. He is the Holy Ghost of God the Father. They all work together for our redemption from sin. We can have hands laid on us in church, and be prayed for to receive, or we may ask the Lord to give us the Holy Ghost as we are on a walk or in our home.

This gift of God is not purchased with money. Peter, one of Jesus' disciples told a man called Simon this as he offered money for the apostles to lay hands on himself to receive the Holy Ghost. It is done by the power of the Lord in us to impart. Be sure your heart is right to receive the Holy Ghost.

Jesus is in our walk in the comfort of Holy Ghost. The Holy Ghost is God. God anointed Jesus of Nazareth with the Holy Ghost, and power. He went around doing good, and healing the oppressed.

The Holy Ghost falls on those who hear and apply The Word of God to their life. When the apostles were teaching the Jews, the Gentiles (us) also received the Holy Ghost as a gift from God. The Jew and the Gentile spoke in other tongues, and magnified God. They were baptized in the Holy Ghost, and then baptized in water in Jesus' Name. Jesus, the Lord said: John the Baptist will baptize you with water, but we (Jesus the Savior, and God the Father) will baptize you with fire (the Holy Ghost) also.

We are to minister in the Lord Jesus with fasting, and praying, and the Holy Ghost will give us guidance from God. That guidance is within us. We will be sent to do God's bidding by the Holy Ghost of God.

Be assembled in one accord, and seek the guidance of the Holy Ghost of God. The Holy Ghost speaks for God. We will have visions to guide us, from God. He will tell us if there are bounds, and afflictions to be dealt with by His Spirit within us. Wait, and pray for direction. Wait for the Lord to move in you.

The Holy Ghost has made overseers to feed the church of God. They are purchased by the blood of the Lamb (Jesus Christ). We should not be ashamed of the hope that the Holy Ghost has put in our hearts. Jesus gave us the Holy Ghost so we would not lose hope of His coming again to receive us to Himself. The love for God is in our hearts by the Holy Ghost.

We are to be praying in the Spirit of the Holy Ghost for the Saints with all supplication. This means with all our heart, earnestly to the Lord God. Put on the helmet of salvation remembering what Jesus did for us on the cross. Take up the shield of faith, and the sword of the Word (our discernment). Gird up your loins with the truth (have the truth in your heart), and put The Gospel of Peace in your walk, and in your conversation.

The Holy Ghost will give us utterance to boldly open our mouth to make known the mystery of The Gospel. We are an ambassador in bonds to Jesus Christ to speak boldly as we ought to speak. Having all we stand in the day of evil.

The Holy Ghost is always in our hearts, and when we are weak in loving another we need to pray in the Holy Spirit. God is in our hearts, and He will guide us in our prayers to help our selfish ways. Our hope is in our hearts. We should never be ashamed because, the love of God is in our hearts. Our strength comes by the Holy Ghost.

The Kingdom of God is not meat, nor drink, but righteousness, peace, and joy in the Holy Ghost (God the Spirit in us). We are acceptable when we serve God in the Holy Ghost. We are to seek peace, and do things that edify others. We will be in harmony, and will be building up, and developing one another.

We are to be ministers for Jesus Christ sanctified by Holy Ghost of God's Spirit. We are to encourage each other to be obedient in word, and deed. The Holy Ghost helps us to speak in words that are not of men's wisdom but, what the Holy Ghost teaches comparing spiritual things with spiritual. Spiritual truths with spiritual languages are from God our Father. This is prophecy, or tongues with the interpretations. Tongues are the evidence of us having the indwelling Spirit of the Holy Ghost. This is God Himself, and His Son Jesus Christ our Savior by their Spirit. These things are not of men's spirit in the world. We have received the Holy Ghost from God, given to us that we might realize, and comprehend, and appreciate the gifts of Divine favor, and blessing so lavishly bestowed on us by God.

● **We have the mind of Christ the Messiah**, and do hold the thoughts (feelings), and purposes of His heart. Our bodies are the temple of the Holy Ghost. We have the indwelling Spirit of God: we are not our own. He is the Holy Ghost in us, and we belong to God in Christ Jesus. We have purity (are innocent), and knowledge by longsuffering, and kindness by the Holy Ghost with patience. We have spiritual insight by love unfeigned (genuine).

We speak The Word of God with the power of God. We have the weapons of righteousness. The right hand attacks and the left hand defends. We are vindicated as truthful, and honest. God is with us as His people. He dwells in us by His Spirit. These are His promises. We are cleansed from the filthiness of the flesh, and spiritually perfected in holiness in the fear of God.

We are to have communion of the Holy Ghost, sharing, and participation of the Holy Ghost in our work for the Lord. This is fellowship, and communion in the presence of the Lord. Grace, and favor come to us in the Lord Jesus, and the love of God the Father. So be it when we preach The Gospel that it goes out in power and in the Holy Ghost with assurance, great conviction, and absolute certainty by each of us. This is a Holy Spirit directed activity. God gives the desire to us to do His work, in the obedience of the prompting of the Holy Ghost. Following the guidance of the Holy Ghost will lead us into a resurrected way of living. Being obedient to the Spirit in simple prompting brings results that are spiritually directed.

We will have the joy of the Holy Ghost. This is the fellowship, and the joy of the presence of God. We can endure affliction by the strength we acquire by praying in the power of the Holy Ghost (our heavenly language). We can be examples for the Lord Jesus Christ in faith, and the love of the Lord Jesus Christ.

We are not called according to our works, but what Jesus did for us to become a part of The Kingdom of God. We were called according to His purpose and by His grace before the world began. Guard with the greatest of care the precious Word of Truth. It was entrusted to us by the help of the Holy Ghost. He is at home living in these mortal bodies. We were washed to regeneration by God's mercy by the renewing of the Holy Ghost/Holy Spirit of God. This was bestowed on us by the sacrifices of Jesus Christ, God's Son. We have new birth in our Savior, Jesus Christ. We are made heirs to the hope of eternal life. We are to renew our minds in Christ Jesus by The Word Who He is.

We are to work by witnessing, and doing signs, and wonders, and different kinds of miracles as the gifts of the Holy Ghost. These things are to be done according to the will of the Holy Ghost. These things are established, and plainly endorsed by God. They are His evidence of approval. **We need to pay attention to these truths or they will pass us by.** They will slip away from us. We must believe in the evidence of speaking in unknown tongues, and the function as evidence of the Holy Ghost by the gifts of God manifestations.

▶ **God set us over the works of His hands.** The Holy Ghost says today: will you hear His Voice? We should worship, bow down, and kneel before God, and let the Holy Ghost move in us. May we not harden our hearts. Humble yourselves in the sight of the Lord, and He will lift you up.

The Holy Ghost is made manifest in us by Jesus Christ so we will be able to enter into the Holy of Holies. We are able to enter into the presence of God. We are a greater more perfect tabernacle not made with hands, but by the Spirit of God in Jesus Christ. The Holy Ghost was sent down by God so we would see the revelation .of God in Christ Jesus.

The Holy Ghost perfects the conscience by cleansing, and the renewing of inner man of the worshiper of God. Prophecy of old and prophecy now comes not of man's will, but by holy men of God speaking as they are empowered by the Holy Ghost. They are moved or, compelled to speak as the Holy Ghost prompts them to do so. The Holy Ghost is one with The Word (Jesus Christ), and our Father God all one bearing witness in Heaven.

We are to build ourselves up in our most holy faith, praying in the Holy Ghost. We receive exceeding joy in the presence of the Lord. He will keep us from falling, and present us faultless before our Father. We are enabled to speak by the empowerment of the

Holy Ghost in due season. We are to believe with all our heart to receive the Holy Ghost. We become the temple of the Holy Ghost of God. The Spirit of God dwells in us.

We are not our own. We were bought with a price. This price is Jesus' death, and resurrection. We are to glorify God Who now lives in our body, and our spirit. We are God's. We are to die to our sins, and serve by God's grace, and mercy. By His great love we are saved. We are raised together, and saved by our faith, and are seated together in heavenly places in Christ Jesus.

We have God's kindness toward us through Jesus Christ. Because of God's great grace we are saved. We are saved through faith, not of ourselves. This is a gift of God. We are a workmanship created to do good works preordained by God to walk in.

• **We are not to be drunk with wine in excess, but are to be filled with the Spirit of God. We are to speak in Psalms, and hymns, and sing spiritual songs. We are to sing, and make melody in our hearts to the Lord.** We are to be filled with the Spirit of Righteousness by Christ Jesus. This brings the glory, and the praise of God. The Holy Ghost moves, and has His being in us. We walk in the Truth, and the Way: Jesus Christ is in us by God's Spirit.

Do not do something to make the Lord regret, be sorrowful, distressed, hurt by grieving the Holy Spirit. This is caused by children of rebellion against the moves of God, and what He wants us to do to glorify Him in our life. Keep His commands, statutes, and love Him with all your heart mind, and soul, and, with all your strength. We want to keep the presence of the Lord God in our midst.

We do not want Him to be sorrowful, regretting all He has done for us by grieving the Holy Spirit. We do not want the Lord God to turn us over to the enemy because of rebellion against the Holy Spirit who is God Himself. He loved, and pitied, carried, redeemed, and lifted Israel up in the days of old. He did this for Israel, and they rebelled, and He turned them over to their enemies. Jesus has come, and redeemed us, and has lifted us up. We must not rebel, and grieve the Holy Spirit. We must honor the name of Jesus Christ always, and be blessed.

★ **God will give His good gift of the Holy Spirit to whomever asks Him.** After we receive the Holy Spirit we are sealed with the Holy Spirit of promise. We have trusted after hearing The Word of Truth. Grieve not the Holy Spirit of God. We are sealed to our day of redemption.

Jesus wants us to forgive others just as He has forgiven us. We are to love one another as God loved man, and gave us Himself in love by the Holy Spirit living in us to the glory of God's only Son Jesus Christ. His indwelling Spirit (The Holy Ghost) will guide us till we all come together. The Jews, God's chosen people and the Gentiles (us) as the adopted children of God for all eternity in God, and with God as a Holy Family forever. All nationalities as believers in God the Father's Son Jesus Christ the Messiah, will make up the Holy Family of God forever.

Notes...

The KINGDOM of GOD

Our Destination Present and Future

The Kingdom of God is not meat or drink, but righteous, peace, and joy in the Holy Ghost. **The Kingdom is within us.** We know the greatness, and the power, and the glory of God. The Spirit of God the Father, and Jesus Christ the Son of God lives in these mortal bodies as we receive and believe. We know no defeat only victory. The Kingdom of God is a Kingdom of priests. It means God is in us, and with us. The spirit of God comes upon us as we receive Jesus Christ as our Savior. It is a relationship between us and God. In Him is victory and majesty. All that is in heaven and earth belong to Jesus Christ the Son of God. His is The Kingdom, and He is to be exalted as head over all. The Kingdom of God is within us. We are the inheritance of Jesus Christ. All who are called a Christian, belong to Jesus Christ. *Every knee shall bow, and every Tongue will confess: "Jesus Christ is Lord of lords". "Jesus Christ is the King of kings".*

Both riches and honor come from Him. He reigns over all. In His hands is the power, and the might. He will make us great, and give us strength. He is to be praised because His great Name brings great tribute to The Kingdom of God. Jesus Christ is, God.

The POWER of GOD

God the Father set up a Kingdom that will never be destroyed. All other kingdoms will not stand. They will be broken, crushed and, consumed. The only nation that will stand is Israel, and we as Christians, believers in Jesus Christ, are spiritual Israel. We are chosen as the adopted children of God because Israel would not receive The Kingdom of God, or except Jesus Christ as the Messiah. We are The Church of Jesus Christ, and with Israel, The Kingdom of God.

The Gentiles (us) believed. A lot of the Jewish nation did not accept Jesus as their King. They crucified their Savior, Jesus Christ. What God says will come to pass and has come to pass. God rules this Kingdom, made up of anyone (mankind) who believes that Jesus Christ is His beloved Son come to save the World. He set over this Kingdom of Heaven 'a man' Who was the humblest and, lowliest of mankind. He is Jesus Christ of Nazareth.

We are all to be wise and have the knowledge to understand these things. God rules the kingdom of mankind and gives it to whomever He wills. We will serve a Messiah, Who will have dominion everlasting not to pass away. His Kingdom is the one that will never be destroyed. God set up His Kingdom which shall never be destroyed. The sovereignty will never be left to any other nation. Israel as a nation will always be the chosen people of God. We as Christians are the brothers and, sisters to Israel forever. We are to pray that Israel will become the nation God wants it to be.

The Kingdom of God under the whole heavens shall be given to us, the people, saints of the Most High God, the Everlasting Kingdom of God. All other dominions shall serve and obey Him. We have to change our minds regretting our sins and change our conduct for our Lord Jesus Christ. We need to change our way of thinking for The Kingdom of God. Jesus Christ will be our kingdom and, the power and, glory forever. We are to be blessed (happy, spiritually prosperous) with life-joy, God's favor and, salvation. Our outward conditions do not count. Ours is The Kingdom of Heaven. We are significant. We are born-again children of God with His unmerited favor, and grace. We enjoy, and find satisfaction in loving and serving God. We are persecuted for doing right. Yet The Kingdom of Heaven is ours in Jesus Christ our Lord.

Our reward in Heaven is great. There in Heaven are all the persecuted prophets before us. We are the salt of the earth and, the light of the world. We are a city on a hill not hidden. There is salvation in and through no one else, only Jesus Christ the Son of God. He lives in us. There is no other name under heaven given among men by which we must be saved.

He who practices the commandments, and teaches them to others shall be called great in The Kingdom of Heaven. We must be in right standing with God. We must have godliness of mind and, character. We will enter into The Kingdom of Heaven with honor, praise, and glorify the Father in Heaven. The Kingdom is God's, by His power, and His glory forever. Seek His Kingdom which is His way of doing things and being righteous or right in your ways. Do not worry. He who does the will of God the Father will enter into The Kingdom of Heaven. Do not act wickedly ignoring His commandments. Be a healthy fruit tree. Be worthy to be admired. Our fruits are our way of being pleasing in the sight of God.

We sit with Abraham, Isaac, and Jacob in The Kingdom of Heaven. We need to preach that The Kingdom of God is at hand. The Kingdom of God is within us. It is Jesus Christ by His spirit. Spread The Good News, The Gospel. John the Baptist is to be admired and is great in God's Kingdom. His fruit was good here on earth. He prepared the way for the coming of Jesus Christ.

The Kingdom of God is within us to drive out evil. The Kingdom of God comes to the one delivered and accepted by repentance, and The Kingdom of God comes upon Him or her. We will know the secrets and mysteries of The Kingdom of Heaven by the knowledge of God in us. It is the Spirit of God in us through Christ Jesus the Son of God and excepting   Him as our Savior. Walk in the Spirit so the enemy cannot steal it from you. Gain understanding and, sew good seed among men to blot out bad seed.

The world will find shelter in The Kingdom of God. The Word will not be suffocated by evil.   The Word is Jesus in us the hope of glory. The Kingdom of God is made of precious seed, (us). We are upright, and in good standing with God. We are trained about The Kingdom of Heaven to be teachers and interpreters of the Sacred Writings of God. We are Disciples for The Kingdom of God. His Kingdom is in us. We are to be shouting for joy and, exaltation as Warriors of Jesus Christ, if we are in The Kingdom of God.

The keys of The Kingdom have been given to us in Christ Jesus, Him living in us. We can bind up the improper and unlawful things on earth. In Jesus' Name we have the power to bind up and loose the power of God on earth, and bind up the powers, and principalities of the air, and evil in high places. They are bound in Heaven. What we declare unlawful on earth is already declared unlawful in Heaven. They pertain to what Jesus has done in earth as it is in Heaven.

We are meek, lowly, loving, and forgiving, and forgiven. We are great in The Kingdom of Heaven-on-earth. He is in us, and around us, and we are in Him. We are the Children of God through Jesus Christ. We welcome the Lord into our life. We must forgive others who sin against us, because Jesus died for the sins of all. The Father has forgiven us forever. We are the Kingdom of God. The Kingdom of Heaven is made up of all God's Children. We are each chosen, and special in His eyes.   Israel is the apple of His eye as a nation.

(Now we are a nation under God in Jesus Christ in America).

The Kingdom of God is Jesus Who would bring us to account for our sins, and forgiven forever. The Kingdom of Heaven is God's estate, and we are the workers in His vineyard. We bring in the harvest for Him. We are the chosen people that will produce for Him. We are invited to the wedding feast of the Lamb of God. The Lamb is Jesus Christ the Messiah.

This Kingdom was prepared for us since the foundation of the world. We are blessed, and favored by God, and appointed the eternal salvation of God. We are to love the Lord with all our heart, mind, and soul, with thought, and understanding, and with all our strength. We are to love our neighbor as our-self.

Jesus is The Kingdom of God in us. Jesus was sent to preach The Good News of The Gospel of The Kingdom of God come, to us. The Kingdom of God is made up of happy children of God. We are filled with life-joy, and satisfaction, and we are favored by God not as our outward condition. We shall laugh even though we are hated. We will be despised because of Jesus in us, the hope of our salvation. We are The Kingdom of God. We must look to the treasures of God to be fit for The Kingdom of God.

We must show forth His might, His power, His majesty, and His magnificence to the world by Jesus Christ in us. Say to sick they are healed when The Kingdom of God is in them. The Kingdom of God is in us; *by His stripes we are healed*. It is God's good pleasure to give us the kingdom. Fear not or be not alarmed. Today we are God's flock, and He watches over us, always. People from the east, west, north, and, south will sit down, and feast together in The Kingdom of God. The Kingdom of God is in within us, among us, and surrounding us. In the day of the Lord's coming we will see flashes of lightning across the whole earth. We will see it from one end of the earth to the other.

What will we do for the sake of The Kingdom of God? The trees will put forth their buds. The Kingdom of God is Jesus coming. The Kingdom of God is in us. Jesus is come to live in us forever. We need to be born again, made new from above. We cannot, without this experience, see or be acquainted with The Kingdom of God. We are to be born of water, baptized, and receive the Holy Spirit of God. We need this experience to enter The Kingdom of God.

Jesus says: My Kingdom (Kingship), His royal power, is not of this world. Jesus is the King, and the truth. Listen to His Voice, The Word. He is The Word of Truth. His Kingdom is righteousness. It makes a person accepted by God. We have a heart of peace, and joy in the Holy Spirit. We serve Jesus Christ as accepted, pleasing to God, and approved by men because we are favored by the Lord our God. We should be in harmony, and build each other up: we should edify, and develop one another in the things of God. We are to build up each other in spiritual things. Our life in The Kingdom of God is based on moral power, and excellence of soul, love and a spirit of gentleness. Unrighteousness or wrongdoing will not inherit The Kingdom of God. We are to be purified, washed clean as in atonement for sin, and made free from the guilt of sin. We are to be consecrated (announced righteous), justified, set apart, trusting in the Name of the Lord Jesus Christ. We are to trust in the Holy Spirit of God.

The Kingdom of God will be all in all, everything to everyone. The Kingdom of God is supreme, the indwelling, and controlling factor of life. We are to die to ourselves, and let Jesus live in us. We cannot be an idolater, and inherit The Kingdom of Christ in God. Our thought-life is to be godliness, pure, and holy, brought under the subjection of Jesus Christ's character living in us. We are The Kingdom of God. Jesus in us; The Hope of Glory. We are delivered out of darkness into His marvelous light, by Him drawing us to Himself.

God the Father, transferred us into The Kingdom of His Son by His love. He has given us redemption through His Blood, and has forgiven us of our sins forever in Him. We are delivered from every assault of evil. We will be brought safely into The Kingdom of God. We have laid up for us a crown of righteousness for being right with God, and doing right. We love Him, and yearn for His glorious return to take us where He is: at the right hand of the Father in Heaven. We will sit down with Him at the Marriage Supper of the Lamb. Jesus is the Lamb. We are His Church. (We have His heart, and He has our heart). We are the Bride of Jesus Christ. We will live with Him forever in The Kingdom of Heaven. Heaven came down, and The Glory of God filled our soul with the love of Jesus Christ our Lord and Savior forever.

by Jerry W. Hollenbeck

• The KINGDOM of GOD
An Agrarian Society

Featuring The Kingdom Realities, Bible Study Course,
Research and Development Classes

• The Word of God
FATHER • WORD • SPIRIT

Literally THE WORD

-----

by Ed Marr

• C. H. P.
The Memoirs of a California Highway Patrol - Badge 9045

----

by Mary Ann England

• Women in Ministry
From her Teachings at the FCF Bible School - Tulsa, Oklahoma
(Foreword by Pat Harrison)

----

by James Jonsten

• WHO is GOD to YOU?
The path to know the most misunderstood name in the universe.

------

by Aaron Jones

• In the SECRET PLACE of THE MOST HIGH
God's Word for Supernatural Healing, Deliverance and Protection

• SOUND from HEAVEN
Praying in Tongues for a Victorious Life

See more Books and all of our products at
www.BoldTruthPublishing.com

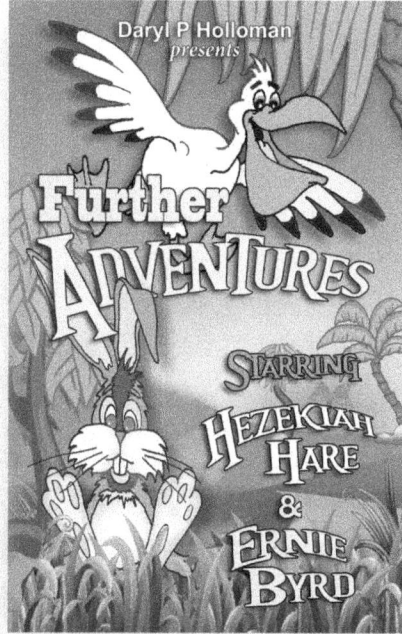

Packed with INSPIRATION
Filled with PRAISE
REFRESHING cover to cover

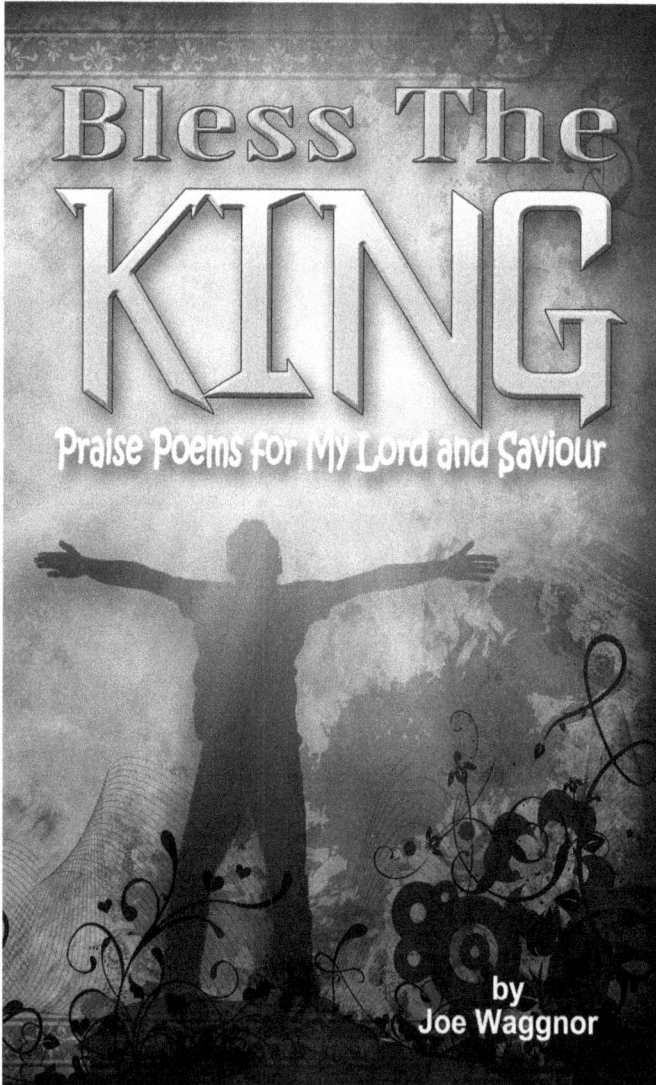

Bless The KING

Praise Poems for My Lord and Saviour

by
Joe Waggnor

A Brand NEW BOOK from
www.BoldTruthPublishing.com